Cookie Dough Delights

More Than 150 Foolproof Recipes for
Cookies, Bars, and Other Treats
Made with Refrigerated Cookie Dough

Camilla V. Saulsbury

CUMBERLAND HOUSE
NASHVILLE, TENNESSEE

To my husband, Kevin

Published by

CUMBERLAND HOUSE PUBLISHING, INC.
431 Harding Industrial Drive
Nashville, Tennessee 37211

Cover design and interior illustrations: JulesRules, Nashville, Tennessee
Text design: Lisa Taylor

Library of Congress Cataloging-in-Publication Data

Saulsbury, Camilla V.
    Cookie dough delights : more than 150 foolproof recipes for cookies, bars, and other treats made with refrigerated cookie dough / Camilla V. Saulsbury
        p. cm.
    Includes index.
    ISBN 1-58182-393-2 (pbk.)
    1. Cookies 2. Refrigerated foods. I. Title.
        TX772.S258 2004
        641.8'654—dc22
                                                                    2004006053

Printed in the United States of America
1 2 3 4 5 6 7 8 — 09 08 07 06 05 04

Contents

Acknowledgments

I am grateful to the many people who helped and encouraged me in the writing of this, my first cookbook: my husband, Kevin, for understanding when all I could talk about was cookies; my parents, Dan and Charlotte, for their endless support and enthusiasm of all my plans; Alan and Donna Spears, for helping me realize what I should be doing and for being my biggest cheerleaders; Ron Pitkin, for taking a chance on my idea; Julie Pitkin, for her wonderful artwork; Lisa Taylor, for making the editing process so smooth; and Brian Powell, my favorite foodie, by far.

Cookie Dough Delights

Introduction

Chocolate chippers, lemon bars, madeleines, brownies, shortbread, thumbprints, rugelach, biscotti, mandelbrot, and fortune cookies—you name them, I love them. And that love only intensifies when the cookies are home-baked. Home-baked cookies are quintessential comfort food, offering instant reassurance, consolation, and community.

I know I am not alone in my cookie adoration. I honestly cannot remember a single occasion when I brought homemade cookies to share—whether for a party, potluck, or meeting—and returned home with more than a crumb-coated plate.

So if we all love cookies, why aren't we baking them more often? Perhaps a lack of essential ingredients when the baking bug strikes, a shortage of time, or even a lingering sense of doubt about baking in general are just three of the impediments that can thwart even the most eager baker/cookie aficionado.

A delicious solution exists, one simple and convenient enough to tempt anyone and everyone back to oven-baked cookie comforts: an assortment of delectable home-baked cookies (and a smattering of other mouth-watering desserts), all of which begin with an 18-ounce roll of refrigerated sugar or chocolate-chip cookie dough from the supermarket dairy case.

With little more than a few easy additions and simple steps, the ordinary can be transformed into the extraordinary. And doing so is all the more enjoyable since the number of steps and ingredients are streamlined and, hence, prep time and cleanup minimized.

It's more than OK to make cookie dough shortcuts. Home bakers have always taken advantage of newly available shortcuts, whether in the form of preshelled and chopped nuts, shredded coconut, pureed pumpkin, measured sticks of butter, or the uniform bits of chocolate we know so well as "chips." In short, making quick, easy and delicious cookies from a roll of refrigerated cookie dough is not about abandoning traditional cookie and dessert recipes but celebrating a host of new options.

Novice bakers, including kids of all ages, will delight in the assured success of working with refrigerated cookie dough, which in turn builds baking confidence and basic cooking skills. Even the most experienced baker gets pinched for time. This book offers a host of simple solutions for such occasions. The speed and ease of working with refrigerated cookie dough also affords bakers of all levels of ability the chance to focus on the aesthetics of cookies and desserts—including fanciful decorations and icings—if they so choose.

So go ahead and get to it. Whether for a picnic, playtime, a grand afternoon with your children, or for no reason at all other than to feel like a kid yourself, a host of delectable cookies and other treats awaits.

If you have any doubt about how delicious these recipes are, cast them aside. Bake a batch of any of these treats to share, pass the plate, and you're bound to hear what every home baker wants to hear: "These are absolutely delicious. May I please have some more?" While you're at it, give them the recipe, too. Happy baking.

Getting Started

A Few Refrigerated Cookie Dough FAQs

If you're an experienced baker, consider these recipes a wonderful enhancement to your existing repertoire, especially when time is at a minimum. It is as much a treat to work with refrigerated cookie dough as it is to eat the sweet results. In general, handle it as you would any other sturdy cookie dough. Below is a quick reference to ensure the best results time and again:

Are the eggs used in refrigerated cookie dough pasteurized?

Yes, the eggs in name-brand and store-brand refrigerated cookie dough are dried and pasteurized.

Can refrigerated cookie dough be eaten raw?

Even though the eggs in the cookie dough are dried and pasteurized, manufacturers do not recommended eating it raw.

Can refrigerated cookie dough be colored with food coloring?

Absolutely. Specific recommendations for types of food coloring and how to use it are discussed in detail at the beginning of Chapter 6. For best results, allow the dough to soften at room temperature, and then work in a small amount of food coloring until well blended. Reshape the dough into a log, wrap tightly in plastic, and refrigerate until firm for best results.

Are there high-altitude adjustments or directions for refrigerated cookie dough?

No, there are no changes for baking refrigerated cookie dough at high altitudes.

Can refrigerated cookie dough be defrosted or prepared in a microwave oven?

No. For best results use a standard, conventional oven or convection oven (for further information about ovens, see page 10). Microwave ovens are inappropriate for cookie baking because the uneven heat prevents the dough from browning and baking evenly.

How should refrigerated cookie dough be stored?

Store unopened cookie dough in the refrigerator. Do not leave cookie dough unrefrigerated for more than two hours. See page 7 for information on freezing cookie dough.

How long can an unopened package of refrigerated cookie dough be stored?

For best quality, use the cookie dough before the use-by date on the package.

Must an entire roll of refrigerated cookie dough be used at once, or can some be used now, some saved for later?

You need not use all of any one roll of refrigerated cookie dough at once; so yes, you can make a few cookies now, and some later. Wrap the unused dough tightly in plastic wrap or in airtight zipper-lock bag and place in the refrigerator or freezer.

For how long can an opened roll of refrigerated cookie dough be stored?

Once opened, refrigerated cookie dough should be used within one week. Use within one month if placed in the freezer after opening.

Do the manufacturers of refrigerated cookie dough recommend adding extra ingredients to refrigerated cookie dough?

Yes. In fact, there is a long history of adding everything from spices, nuts, and dried fruit to chocolate chips, candy, and toffee brickle.

Introduction

Can refrigerated cookie dough be stored once ingredients have been added?

Yes. Tightly wrap the dough in plastic wrap or in an airtight zipper-lock bag and place in the refrigerator or freezer. Use dough within one week if placed in refrigerator and within one month if stored in the freezer.

Can refrigerated cookie dough be rolled and cut out with cookie cutters?

Yes, you can roll and cut sugar cookie dough (*see* Basic Rolled Sugar Cookies, page 62). However, rolling chocolate-chip dough is not recommended—the chips make it difficult to roll. Moreover, the chips melt while baking, distorting the cut-out shapes.

Can refrigerated cookie dough be frozen?

Yes. Freeze unopened rolls of refrigerated cookie dough in the freezer for two to four months. For best results, freeze the dough before the use-by date on the package.

What is the recommended method for thawing frozen rolls of refrigerated cookie dough?

Place frozen rolls of refrigerated cookie dough in the refrigerator and thaw overnight. Microwave thawing is not recommended.

Can the cookies in this book be frozen after baking?

Yes, see page 17 for information on storing cookies. How to freeze depends on the type of cookie (e.g., bar cookies whole, drop cookies in a freezer bag).

Does it matter which brand of refrigerated cookie dough is used for the recipes in this book?

No, it does not. So long as it is an 18-ounce roll, any of the major brands or store brands may be used for these recipes. The recipes in this book were tested using Pillsbury, Nestlé, and several store brands of sugar and chocolate-chip refrigerated cookie dough. Let your own tastebuds determine your preferred brand.

Before You Bake

A Time and a Place for Cookies

I love to make, eat, and share cookies. But if an award for impatience existed—particularly one associated with waiting for sweets—I would win, hands down.

We've all been there at one time or another. It's ten minutes before bedtime and you remember you promised to bring a batch of cookies to the coworker pitch-in tomorrow morning. Or your eight-year-old suddenly recalls he committed you to bring two batches of your "amazing home-baked cookies, Mom!" to this week's Cub Scout meeting—and the twenty hungry boys are due to assemble in an hour. Or you get the irrepressible urge to bake up some warm, crispy-gooey chocolate chippers before you settle down to read a few precious pages of that great new book you're reading.

In my own case, such scenarios have led to such masterpieces as "blackened cookies" (lovingly dubbed by my husband), the saltiest lemon bars the world has ever known, and grey snickerdoodles (don't ask—it's still a mystery).

Hence my advice: take your time. Relax. Enjoy. Change into something comfortable, don your favorite frayed apron, slip into a pair of comfortable shoes, and pour yourself a cup of tea. Better still, invite your children or a good friend into the kitchen to share in the simple pleasure of cookie creation.

The good news is that, because premade cookie dough makes all of these recipes quick and easy, you will have more time for the really fun part: giving the cookie dough your own special touch, whether it's a simple stir-in of toffee bits and pecans, a delicious squiggle of icing, a fanciful white chocolate dip, or an easy but amazing transformation from cookie dough to cobbler, torte, or cheesecake.

The hardest part may be deciding which treat to make first. But once your choice is made, clear off some counter space, read through the recipe in its entirety, and assemble the necessary ingredients and equipment. Prepare the pans and soften or bring to room temperature any ingredients that require it. Next, preheat the oven (unless the dough requires chilling time after mixing). That's it!

The Best Baking Investment You May Ever Make: An Oven Thermometer

If I could stand on my soapbox and make a single plea to home bakers it would be this: buy an oven thermometer to check your oven temperature. Unless you have a state-of-the-art oven (and even then, temperature discrepancies can still occur), it is very likely that your oven temperature is inaccurate. It may be off as few as five degrees or as many as fifty degrees, but whatever the discrepancy, it will affect your results.

The good news is that an easy, inexpensive, readily available remedy exists: an oven thermometer. You can find this simple tool in the baking section of most supermarkets or superstores (e.g., Kmart, Target, and Wal-Mart), kitchen stores, and hardware stores (typically if they have a pots and pans section they will carry oven thermometers). They are well under ten dollars.

Once purchased, simply place or attach the oven thermometer in your oven (see package instructions) and preheat. Once your oven indicates that it has reached the temperature setting, check your oven thermometer. If the oven temperature is higher on the thermometer than the setting you selected, you will need to set your oven that many degrees lower. For example, if the thermometer reads 375° and you had set your oven for 350°, you know that you will need to set your oven to 325° in the future for it to reach 350°. Leave the oven thermometer in the oven and check it every time you preheat the oven to monitor temperature accuracy.

While few ovens are precise, most are consistent. That is, if it is 25 degrees hotter than the selected temperature, it tends to stay 25 degrees too hot all of the time. This may shift slightly at extremely high temperatures (exceeding 400°). However, temperatures lower than 400° are used for all of the baking recipes in this book.

Know Thy Oven

Whether used a little or a lot, it is worth taking a few minutes to familiarize yourself with your oven's myriad functions. Some ovens have specialty features specific to baking, such as precision temperature settings and extra-large interior capacities that allow for multiple items baking at once, so take advantage of these for delicious baked results. Also, give the interior a good cleaning. This is especially important if you have no idea when it last got a thorough wipe-down or if you recently baked or roasted something particularly aromatic. Lingering odors or scents can alter the flavor and smell of your cookies and desserts.

The three most common types of baking ovens for the home kitchen are conventional (gas or electric), convection, and toaster.

Conventional

This is the most common type of oven. All of the recipes in this book were tested using a standard, conventional oven. The heat source is located in the bottom of conventional ovens, allowing for the heat to rise up through the oven in a more or less even manner.

Convection

By contrast, the heat source in a convection oven is located behind the oven wall. In addition, convection ovens have a fan that continuously circulates air through the oven cavity. When hot air is blowing onto food, as opposed to merely surrounding it (as in a conventional oven), the food tends to cook more quickly and evenly, ideal for baking perfect, evenly browned cookies. The circulating air may alter the amount of time needed for baking, so you may need to do a small experimental batch to get a sense of how to adjust the baking time.

Toaster

I do not recommend baking any of the cookies or other desserts in this book in a toaster oven. The exception to this rule is the more recent combination toaster/convection ovens that have appeared on the market in the last few years. These ovens offer more even circulation of heat than traditional toaster ovens. Drop cookies are the best option for baking small batches of cookies in these ovens, but follow the manufacturer's guidelines for adapting recipe baking times.

Essential Utensils

- Dry measuring cups in graduated sizes $\frac{1}{4}$, $\frac{1}{3}$, $\frac{1}{2}$, and 1 cup
- Liquid measuring cup (preferably clear glass or plastic)
- Measuring spoons in graduated sizes $\frac{1}{4}$, $\frac{1}{2}$, and 1 teaspoon as well as 1 tablespoon
- Wooden spoon(s)
- Mixing bowls (at least one each of small, medium, and large sizes)
- Rubber or silicone spatula (for scraping the sides of a mixing bowl)
- Metal spatula or pancake turner for removing cookies from sheets (or plastic if you are using a nonstick-coated pan)
- Wire cooling racks
- Oven mitts or holders
- Kitchen timer
- Pastry brush (a cleaned 1–inch paintbrush from the hardware store works fine)
- Rolling pin (only for a few recipes)
- Wire whisk

- Chef's knife
- Kitchen spoons (everyday place setting soup and teaspoons for drop cookies)
- Electric mixer (handheld or stand mixer)

Wish-List Utensils
- Cookie scoops (look like small ice cream scoops—use for perfectly measured drop cookies)
- Food processor
- Cookie cutters
- Silicone cookie sheet liners (eliminates non-stick spray or greasing step)
- Zester
- Metal icing spatula
- Melon baller (for making perfect thumbprint cookie impressions)

Pans
- Aluminum cookie sheets (at least two)
- 8-inch square pan
- 9-inch square pan
- Jelly roll pan (10 x 15 inches)
- Standard 12-cup muffin pan
- Miniature muffin pan
- Madeleine pan
- Deep-dish pie pan (9-inch)
- Springform pan (9- or 10-inch)

Measure for Measure

How to Measure Dry Ingredients

When measuring a dry ingredient such as sugar, flour, spices, or salt, spoon it into the appropriate-size dry measuring cup or measuring spoon, heaping it up over the top. Next, slide a straight-edged utensil, such as a knife, across the top to level off the extra. Be careful not to shake or tap the cup or spoon to settle the ingredient or you will have more than you need.

How to Measure Liquid Ingredients

Use a clear plastic or glass container with lines up the sides to measure liquid ingredients. Set the container on the counter and pour the liquid to the appropriate mark. Lower your head to read the measurement at eye level.

How to Measure Moist Ingredients

Some moist ingredients, such as brown sugar, coconut, and dried fruits, must be firmly packed into the measuring cup to be measured accurately. Use a dry measuring cup for these ingredients. Fill the measuring cup to slightly overflowing, then pack down the ingredient firmly with the back of a spoon. Add more of the ingredient and pack down again until the cup is full and even with the top of the measure.

Time to Bake

Preheating the Oven

For perfectly baked cookies, preheat the oven, which takes about ten to fifteen minutes, depending on your oven.

Center of the Oven

If baking just one sheet or pan of cookies at a time, place it on a rack set in the center of the oven and change from back to front halfway through the baking cycle. Leave at least two inches of space on all sides between the edge of the sheet and the oven walls for proper air circulation.

Two Sheets at a Time: Switch the Racks

It's okay to bake more than one sheet of cookies at a time. Use the upper and lower thirds of the oven, reversing sheets from upper to lower and front to back about halfway through the baking period to ensure even baking. Even the best ovens can build up hot spots in certain areas.

Keep in mind, too, that two sheets of cookies in the oven may require a slightly longer baking time than one sheet. One of the pans may be ready sooner than the other. Reverse the pans in the oven for evenly baked cookies.

Checking for Doneness

Bake cookies the minimum amount of time, even though the center may look slightly underbaked. To check cookies for doneness, press down lightly in the middle to see if it bounces back. Bake sliced cookies until the edges are firm and the bottoms are lightly browned. Generally, cookies are done when the edges begin to brown, or when they are golden. Every pan bakes differently, depending on the material, thickness, weight, and surface reflection.

Remember to open and close the oven door quickly to maintain the proper baking temperature.

Most importantly, watch carefully, especially batches of individual cookies that bake for very short amounts of time. While a watched pot may never boil, unwatched cookies will likely burn.

Cooling Cookie Sheets in between Batches

Always cool the cookie sheet before baking another batch. A warm pan causes the dough to melt which can cause overspreading, deformed cookies, or altered baking times. To cool cookie sheets quickly between baking, rinse under cold water until the sheet is completely cooled. Dry and proceed with the next batch of cookies.

Cooling

Remove baked cookies immediately from the cookie sheet with a wide spatula, unless the recipe states other cooling directions. Place cookies in a single layer on wire racks to cool evenly, so the bottoms don't get soggy. You can transfer some cookies immediately to the wire racks, while others need a couple minutes to cool on the cookie sheet. If the cookie bends or breaks when transferring, wait another minute before trying. Thoroughly cool cookies before storing them to prevent them from becoming soggy.

A Few Words about Cookie Sheets

People have strong ideas about their preferred cookie sheet, so consider the following recommendations as guidelines rather than inflexible rules. I find that the more information I have about the baking process, the easier it is to "foolproof" recipes. For example, knowing that different sheets and pans can produce different results, and why, can reduce the possibility of your favorite recipe tasting wonderful one time, okay the next, and positively inedible on the occasion you plan to share it at a potluck party.

When baking cookies, choose light-colored, dull-finished, heavy-gauge cookie sheets. Shiny sheets work best for cookies that should not brown too much on the bottom.

Except for bar cookies, avoid using cookie sheets with high sides. Such pans can deflect heat as well as make it difficult to remove the cookies for cooling. As a general rule, cookie sheets should be two inches narrower and shorter than the oven to allow for even baking.

It is best to avoid dark aluminum cookie sheets. These sheets have a brown or almost black finish and may absorb heat, causing bottoms of cookies to brown more quickly. If using these sheets is the only option, decrease the baking time and lower the temperature slightly (about 25°).

Nonstick cookie sheets are easier to clean and help ensure even baking; however, the dough may not spread as much and you may end up with a thicker cookie. On the other hand, rich cookies can spread if baked on a greased sheet. Follow the manufacturer's instructions if using a cookie sheet with a nonstick coating; the oven temperature may need to be reduced by 25°.

Also follow the manufacturer's instructions if using insulated cookie sheets, which are made from two sheets of metal with a layer of air between for insulation. Cookies will not brown as much on the bottom, so it may hard to tell when the cookies are done. Also, cookies may take slightly longer to bake.

If you don't have enough cookie sheets, you can invert a jelly roll pan or use heavy-duty foil.

Quick Cookie Sheet Q&A: Why Do Cookies Stick?

If cookies stick, it is most likely due to one of the following, and easily remedied, problems:

- The cookie sheets were not sufficiently cleaned between uses.
- The cookie sheets were not greased or sprayed with nonstick spray and the recipe called for greasing or spraying.
- The cookies were underbaked.
- The cookies were left on cookie sheets too long before removal.
- The cookie batter was too warm.
- The cookie sheets were warm or hot before baking.

Storing Cookies

Once cookies are baked, keep them delicious by taking care with their storage. Most importantly, store them in an airtight container for optimal freshness. Sturdier cookies, such as drop cookies, can be place in a zippered plastic bag, but more delicate filled and formed cookies are better off stacked between layers of wax paper in a plastic container.

Bar cookies can be stacked in a container between layers of wax paper or stored in their baking pan. I prefer to cut them first and then place them back in the pan for easy removal. Cover the top tightly with aluminum foil, wrap, or a lid. For delicate, crisp cookies, store in a sturdy container such as a cookie jar or tin.

Lay extra-fragile cookies flat in a wide container with parchment or wax paper between the layers. If you have iced or decorated cookies, let them dry before storing. (If freezing, freeze on a pan in a single layer, and then carefully stack layers with wax paper between layers).

Freezing Already Baked Cookies

To enjoy your cookies for several weeks, or even months, freeze them. For best results, freeze the cookies as soon as possible after they are completely cooled. Both individual and bar cookies can be frozen with equal success. With either type, it is best to frost at a future date when the cookies have been thawed. Place the cookies in freezer bags or airtight freezer containers for up to 6 to 12 months. Double wrap cookies to prevent them from getting freezer burn or absorbing odors from the freezer. Label the cookies clearly with the name of the cookie and the date. Cookies can be frosted after thawing at room temperature for 15 minutes.

Shipping Cookies

A care package full of home-baked cookies? It may be the best gift ever. To insure perfect delivery, consider the following tips:

(1) Biscotti, bar, and drop cookies can best withstand mailing; tender, fragile cookies are apt to crumble when shipped. Line a heavy cardboard box, cookie tin, or empty coffee can with aluminum foil or plastic wrap. Wrap four to six cookies of the same size together in aluminum foil, plastic wrap, or plastic food bags and seal securely with tape; repeat until the container is full.

(2) Place the heaviest cookies at the bottom of the container and layer the wrapped cookies with bubble wrap or crumpled paper towels. Use either of these to line the container. Seal the container with tape.

(3) Put the container (tin, coffee can, etc.) into a sturdy cardboard box. Use bubble wrap or newspaper to protect the container.

(4) Print the mailing address and return address on the package in waterproof ink; mark the package "PERISHABLE FOOD" to encourage quick and careful handling. Choose overnight shipping.

(5) Wrap different cookie varieties in plastic wrap and divide layers with waxed paper. Use crumpled or shredded paper towels or plastic bubble wrap inside the container for padding. Seal the container with tape.

(6) To insure that cookies arrive in the best possible condition, carefully pack them between layers of waxed paper in a rigid tin. Use crumpled waxed paper to fill in any extra space. Pack this tin in a larger, sturdy shipping box. Pad the area around the box with crumpled paper or other packing material, seal and address.

(7) If cookie cutters are used to make cut-out, decorated cookies, use smaller design cutters—they are less likely to break in transit than larger cookies.

(8) Cool cookies completely before storing or they will get soft and sticky.

(9) To keep flavors from changing or blending with others, pack cookies in separate containers or wrap the different types separately within a container.

1 Drop Cookies

Drop cookies are just that, cookies made from spoonfuls of dough dropped onto a cookie sheet. Think of chocolate-chip, oatmeal raisin, and peanut butter cookies, and you know drop cookies. Most of my favorite cookies from childhood—and most likely yours, too—fit into this yummy category. Maybe it's because these were the first cookies that I was able to "assist" my mother in the production, from mixing in chocolate chips, raisins, or oats to spooning up blobs of the delicious dough with a few kitchen teaspoons. Maybe it was just because they were the homiest cookies, typically lumpy-bumpy and perfect with a cold glass of milk or a warm mug of cocoa.

Whatever the case, drop cookies are typically the simplest cookies to make and bake. And when you start with refrigerated cookie dough, they are that much easier. With a short list of ingredients (some recipes as few as two) and some wielding of a wooden spoon, a range of homey, fresh-from-the-oven cookies—both classics and exciting new twists—is only minutes away.

Mocha Chocolate-Chip Cookies

If food marriages are made in heaven, then surely chocolate-coffee is one of the select matches. Given how the two flavors bring out the best in each other, you will be hard-pressed finding someone to turn down an offer of one or more of these cookies. More likely, you will need to conceal a stash for yourself before they evaporate into thin air.

- 1 18-ounce roll refrigerated chocolate-chip cookie dough
- 1½ teaspoons vanilla extract
- 2½ teaspoons instant espresso (or coffee) powder
- 2 tablespoons unsweetened cocoa powder
- ½ teaspoon ground cinnamon

Preheat oven to 350°. Spray cookie sheets with nonstick cooking spray.

Break up cookie dough into large bowl; let stand 10–15 minutes to soften.

In a small cup combine the vanilla and espresso powder. Add vanilla mixture, cocoa powder, and cinnamon to the cookie dough; mix well with your fingers, the paddle attachment of an electric stand mixer, or a wooden spoon.

Drop dough by kitchen teaspoons, two inches apart, onto prepared cookie sheets.

Bake 10–13 minutes or until just set and golden at edges. Transfer cookies to wire racks and cool completely.

Makes 28 cookies.

Frosted Double-Apricot Drop Cookies

If you are not already an apricot lover, you will be converted—instantly—after tasting these fruit-packed gems.

1   18-ounce roll refrigerated sugar cookie dough
1   3-ounce package cream cheese, cut into bits
1   cup chopped dried apricots
1   cup boiling water
1   recipe Apricot Frosting, see page 207

Preheat oven to 350°. Spray cookie sheets with nonstick cooking spray.

Break up cookie dough into large bowl; add cream cheese to bowl and let stand 10–15 minutes to soften. In a small bowl place the apricots with boiling water and let stand 10–15 minutes. Drain apricots and pat dry with paper towels.

Add dried apricots to bowl with cream cheese and cookie dough; mix well with your fingers, the paddle attachment of an electric stand mixer, or a wooden spoon.

Drop dough by kitchen teaspoons, two inches apart, onto prepared cookie sheets.

Bake 10–13 minutes or until just set and golden at edges. Transfer cookies to wire racks and cool completely. Frost with Apricot Frosting.

Makes 28 cookies.

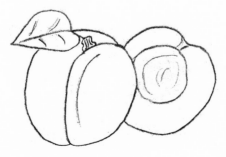

Drop Cookies

Toffee Apple Cookies

My better half, Kevin, is such a cookie lover that he prefers a fresh-baked batch to birthday cake. I'm happy to oblige him with these easy drop cookies inspired by one of my favorite confections.

1	18-ounce roll refrigerated sugar cookie dough
1	6-ounce package dried apples, chopped
¾	cup English toffee baking bits
1	recipe Chocolate Dip/Drizzle, see page 201, (optional)

Preheat oven to 350°. Spray cookie sheets with nonstick cooking spray.

Break up cookie dough into large bowl; let stand 10–15 minutes to soften. Add dried apples and toffee bits; mix well with your fingers, the paddle attachment of an electric stand mixer, or a wooden spoon.

Drop dough by kitchen teaspoons, two inches apart, onto prepared cookie sheets.

Bake 10–13 minutes or until just set and golden at edges. Transfer cookies to wire racks and cool completely.

If desired, dunk one end of each cookie into Chocolate Dip; place dipped cookies on waxed paper–lined cookie sheet. Place cookies in refrigerator until chocolate is set.

> Baker's Note: These cookies are outstanding dipped or drizzled in any variety of chocolate—semisweet, white, or milk chocolate. It's your call!

Makes 32 cookies.

Chocolate-Chip Raisin Cookies

These are exceptional cookies—in taste, time, brevity of ingredients, and absolute ease of preparation. They taste just like a big box of chocolate-covered raisins, all wrapped up in brown sugar-y dough. While chocolate-raisin is a classic combination, you can substitute other dried fruit—dried cranberries, golden raisins, chopped tropical fruit bits, chopped apricots, or cranberries—for an equally tasty variation.

- 1 18-ounce roll refrigerated chocolate-chip cookie dough
- 1 cup raisins
- ½ teaspoon ground cinnamon

- Preheat oven to 350°. Spray cookie sheets with nonstick cooking spray.

- Break up cookie dough into large bowl; let stand 10–15 minutes to soften. Add raisins and cinnamon; mix well with your fingers, the paddle attachment of an electric stand mixer, or a wooden spoon.

- Drop dough by kitchen teaspoons, two inches apart, onto prepared cookie sheets.

- Bake 10–13 minutes or until just set and golden at edges. Transfer cookies to wire racks and cool completely.

Makes 30 cookies.

Cinnamon Pecan Cookies

Nothing beats the undeniable comfort and unmistakable flavor of cinnamon. It's hard to believe that this rich and homey cookie comes together with such ease. Pecans add a nutty sweetness, but almonds or walnuts can substitute if that's what you have on hand.

- **1   18-ounce roll refrigerated sugar cookie dough**
- **2   teaspoons cinnamon**
- **½   teaspoon ground nutmeg**
- **2   teaspoons vanilla extract**
- **1½ cups chopped pecans**

Preheat oven to 350°. Spray cookie sheets with nonstick cooking spray.

Break up cookie dough into large bowl; let stand 10–15 minutes to soften. Add cinnamon, nutmeg, vanilla, and pecans; mix well with your fingers, the paddle attachment of an electric stand mixer, or a wooden spoon.

Drop dough by kitchen teaspoons, two inches apart, onto prepared cookie sheets.

Bake 10–13 minutes or until just set and golden at edges. Remove from oven and cool on baking sheets for 2 minutes; transfer to wire racks and cool completely.

Makes 28 cookies.

Lemon-Ginger White Chocolate Softies

One of my lemon-loving friends informs me that these soft and tender cookies are now near the top of her list of all-time favorite cookies. Combining the cookie dough with the cream cheese could not be easier—just be sure to soften the cream cheese to room temperature for easy mixing. A wooden spoon will work, but for best results, use an electric mixer. If you have a stand mixer, opt for the paddle attachment.

1	18-ounce roll refrigerated sugar cookie dough
1	8-ounce package cream cheese, softened
1	tablespoon grated lemon zest
2	teaspoons ground ginger
1	cup white chocolate chips
1	recipe Lemon Icing, see page 204

Preheat oven to 350°. Spray cookie sheets with nonstick cooking spray.

Break up cookie dough into large bowl; let stand 10–15 minutes to soften. Add cream cheese, lemon zest, and ginger. Mix well with an electric mixer on medium speed until well combined. Add white chocolate chips; mix well with a wooden spoon.

Drop dough by kitchen teaspoons, two inches apart, onto prepared cookie sheets.

Bake 10–13 minutes or until just set and golden at edges. Quickly transfer cookies to wire racks and cool completely. If desired, drizzle with Lemon Icing.

Makes 40 cookies.

Buttered Rum Raisin Cookies

One of my favorite college professors loved to bake. He made the best breads and cookies and, lucky for me and his other students, often brought the results of his late-night baking experiments to class for all of us to enjoy. As an added bonus, he also shared his recipes. This is an adaptation of one of his (and now my) favorites. Delicious plain, they are positively scrumptious frosted with a rum-laced browned butter icing.

1   18-ounce roll refrigerated sugar cookie dough
1   cup raisins
1   recipe Butter-Rum Icing, see page 210

Preheat oven to 350°. Spray cookie sheets with nonstick cooking spray.

Break up cookie dough into large bowl; let stand 10–15 minutes to soften. Add raisins; mix well with your fingers, the paddle attachment of an electric stand mixer, or a wooden spoon.

Drop dough by kitchen teaspoons, two inches apart, onto prepared cookie sheets.

Bake 10–13 minutes or until just set and golden at edges. Immediately remove from cookie sheets; place on wire racks.

Spoon about 1 teaspoon Butter-Rum Icing over each warm cookie. If icing becomes too thick, reheat over low heat.

Makes 28 cookies.

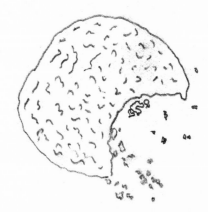

Drop Cookies

Coconut Macaroonies

I don't know whether "nature" or "nurture" best explains why my mother and I share the same dessert preferences. Whatever the reason, our mutual confection affections sure make our time together all the sweeter. We both love macaroons, whether they are crispy or chewy. This simple version is both—crispy at the edges, chewy toward the center. Find coconut extract where you find vanilla extract in the baking section of the supermarket. It really adds "oomph" to the flavor of these cookies.

1   **18-ounce roll refrigerated sugar cookie dough**
1   **3-ounce package cream cheese, softened**
1½ **teaspoons coconut extract (or vanilla extract)**
1   **7-ounce package shredded coconut**

- Preheat oven to 350°. Spray cookie sheets with nonstick cooking spray.

- Break up cookie dough into large bowl; let stand 10–15 minutes to soften. Add cream cheese and extract. Mix well with an electric mixer on medium speed until well combined. Add coconut; mix well with a wooden spoon.

- Drop dough by kitchen teaspoons, two inches apart, onto prepared cookie sheets.

- Bake 10–13 minutes or until just set and golden at edges. Quickly transfer cookies to wire racks and cool completely.

Makes 36 cookies.

Giant Chocolate-Chip Cranberry Oatmeal Cookies

I suppose plain oatmeal cookies are fine, but I am of the mindset that "more is more" when it comes to cookies. Loaded with chocolate chips and dried cranberries, these fit the bill, beautifully. They make great travelers, too, whether across town or across the country.

1	18-ounce roll refrigerated chocolate-chip cookie dough
1	teaspoon ground cinnamon
⅔	cup old-fashioned or quick oats
⅔	cup chopped dried cranberries (or tart cherries)

• Preheat oven to 350°. Spray cookie sheets with nonstick cooking spray.

• Break up cookie dough into large bowl; let stand 10–15 minutes to soften. Add cinnamon, oats, and cranberries; mix well with wooden spoon or fingers just until combined (dough will be stiff).

• Drop dough by rounded ¼ cupfuls, two inches apart, onto prepared cookie sheet. Flatten to ½-inch thickness.

• Bake 13–18 minutes or until cookies are slightly puffed and edges are golden brown. Cool 1 minute. Transfer to wire racks and cool completely.

Makes 9 giant cookies.

Double-Chip Chippers

Sweet tooth that I am, I always feel that most chocolate-chip cookie recipes have too much cookie and not enough chips. This recipe remedies the problem. I guarantee a hearty dose of gooey goodness in every bite.

1	**18-ounce roll refrigerated chocolate-chip cookie dough**
¾	**cup milk chocolate, white chocolate, peanut butter, cinnamon, or butterscotch chips**

Preheat oven to 350°. Spray cookie sheets with nonstick cooking spray.

Break up cookie dough into large bowl; let stand 10–15 minutes to soften. Add the baking chips; mix well with your fingers, the paddle attachment of an electric stand mixer, or a wooden spoon.

Drop dough by kitchen teaspoons, two inches apart, onto prepared cookie sheets.

Bake 10–13 minutes or until just set and golden at edges. Transfer cookies to wire racks and cool completely.

Makes 28 cookies.

Drop Cookies

Double-Chip Chippers

Cinnamon-Orange Chocolate Chippers

Perhaps it's time to modify the old adage "As American as apple pie." By my measure, it's chocolate-chip cookies that most fittingly define dessert "Americana" these days. Here a lively dose of cinnamon and orange zest lends everyone's favorite cookie a subtly spicy, citrus edge.

1   18-ounce roll refrigerated chocolate-chip cookie dough
1¼ teaspoons ground cinnamon
1   tablespoon grated orange zest

●Preheat oven to 350°. Spray cookie sheets with nonstick cooking spray.

●Break up cookie dough into large bowl; let stand 10–15 minutes to soften. Add the cinnamon and orange zest; mix well with your fingers, the paddle attachment of an electric stand mixer, or a wooden spoon.

●Drop dough by kitchen teaspoons, two inches apart, onto prepared cookie sheets.

●Bake 10–13 minutes or until just set and golden at edges. Transfer cookies to wire racks and cool completely.

Makes 24 cookies.

Chocolate-Chip Cocoa Cookies

If chocolate chip cookies are wonderful, then these chocolate-chocolate-chip cookies are sublime. If you want to take them all the way over the top, consider dipping or drizzling the cooled cookies in the Chocolate Dip or Drizzle on page 201.

1   18-ounce roll refrigerated chocolate-chip cookie dough
2   tablespoons unsweetened cocoa powder
1½ teaspoons vanilla extract

- Preheat oven to 350°. Spray cookie sheets with nonstick cooking spray.

- Break up cookie dough into large bowl; let stand 10–15 minutes to soften. Add cocoa powder and vanilla to the cookie dough; mix well with your fingers, the paddle attachment of an electric stand mixer, or a wooden spoon.

- Drop dough by kitchen teaspoons, two inches apart, onto prepared cookie sheets.

- Bake 10–13 minutes or until just set in the centers. Transfer cookies to wire racks and cool completely.

Makes 24 cookies.

Drop Cookies

Key Lime Cookies

These cookies have a marvelous flavor with a bright citrus edge that's just tart enough to nicely offset the richness of the sugar cookie dough. You can substitute lemon or orange for the lime.

- 1   **18-ounce roll refrigerated sugar cookie dough**
- 1   **tablespoon grated lime zest**
- 1   **recipe Lime Icing, see page 204**

Preheat oven to 350°. Spray cookie sheets with nonstick cooking spray.

Break up cookie dough into large bowl; let stand 10–15 minutes to soften. Add lime zest; mix well with your fingers, the paddle attachment of an electric stand mixer, or a wooden spoon.

Drop dough by kitchen teaspoons, two inches apart, onto prepared cookie sheets.

Bake 10–13 minutes or until just set and golden at edges. Transfer cookies to wire racks and cool completely. Drizzle with Lime Icing.

Makes 24 cookies.

Carrot Cake Cookie Jumbles

Restraint is a concept I refuse to associate with cookies. Hence "jumble" cookies—baked goodies chock full of all sorts of yummy ingredients—suit me to a T. These carrot-y cookies are moist and flavorful, just like a slice or square of homemade carrot cake. For the "icing on the cake," add icing to the cookie—specifically, Cream Cheese Frosting.

1	18-ounce roll refrigerated chocolate-chip cookie dough (or sugar cookie dough)
1	8-ounce package cream cheese, softened
2	cups peeled, shredded carrots
2	cups shredded coconut
1	cup dried raisins (or cranberries)
1	teaspoon ground cinnamon
1	recipe Cream Cheese Frosting, see page 208, (optional)

Preheat oven to 350°. Spray cookie sheets with nonstick cooking spray.

Break up cookie dough into large bowl; let stand 10–15 minutes to soften. Add cream cheese. Mix well with an electric mixer on medium speed until well combined. Add carrots, coconut, raisins, and cinnamon; mix well with a wooden spoon.

Drop dough by kitchen teaspoons, two inches apart, onto prepared cookie sheets.

Bake 10–13 minutes or until just set and golden at edges. Quickly transfer cookies to wire racks and cool completely. If desired, frost with Cream Cheese Frosting.

Makes 48 cookies.

Piña Colada Pineapple Drops

Pineapple and coconut create a fresh burst of flavor for this harmonious little cookie. For some added crunch, stir in ½ cup of chopped macadamia nuts or blanched almonds. For a beautiful summer dessert platter, serve them up surrounded by a sliced assortment of the season's finest fruit.

> 1 **18-ounce roll refrigerated sugar cookie dough**
> ¾ **cup chopped dried pineapple**
> ¾ **cup shredded coconut**
> 1½ **teaspoons rum flavor (or vanilla extract)**

- Preheat oven to 350°. Spray cookie sheets with nonstick cooking spray.

- Break up cookie dough into large bowl; let stand 10–15 minutes to soften. Add dried pineapple, coconut, and extract; mix well with your fingers, the paddle attachment of an electric stand mixer, or a wooden spoon.

- Drop dough by kitchen tea-spoons, two inches apart, onto prepared cookie sheets.

- Bake 10–13 minutes or until just set and golden at edges. Transfer cookies to wire racks and cool completely.

Makes 28 cookies.

White Chocolate Peppermint Snowdrops

When I moved from California to the Midwest to attend graduate school, I found myself longing for a winter-wonderful cookie to spur me on through gray, slushy December and January weather. These easy treats quickly became my hot cocoa companions.

1　18-ounce roll refrigerated sugar cookie dough
1⅓ cups white chocolate chips
1　recipe Peppermint Icing, see page 213
1　cup crushed peppermint candies (or candy canes)

Preheat oven to 350°. Spray cookie sheets with nonstick cooking spray.

Break up cookie dough into large bowl; let stand 10–15 minutes to soften. Add white chocolate chips; mix well with your fingers, the paddle attachment of an electric stand mixer, or a wooden spoon.

Drop dough by measuring tablespoonfuls onto prepared cookie sheets.

Bake 10–13 minutes or until just set and golden at edges. Cool 2 minutes; transfer to wire racks and cool completely. Drizzle cookies with Peppermint Icing and sprinkle with crushed peppermint candies.

Baker's Note: To crush the peppermint candies, place in a small, zippered plastic bag. Cover bag with dishtowel and pound with a meat mallet, rolling pin, or soup can.

Makes 28 cookies.

Drop Cookies

White Chocolate Peppermint

Banana-Chip Chippers

No monkey business here, just a bunch of delicious chocolate-chip cookies with a welcome new crunch of flavor. You can find banana chips in one or more places in the supermarket: the health food section, the dried fruits section, or in the bulk foods section. If you cannot find them there, a health food store is sure to sell them.

1   18-ounce roll refrigerated chocolate-chip cookie dough
1¼ cups crushed banana chips

- Preheat oven to 350°. Spray cookie sheets with nonstick cooking spray.

- Break up cookie dough into large bowl; let stand 10–15 minutes to soften. Add banana chips; mix well with your fingers, the paddle attachment of an electric stand mixer, or a wooden spoon.

- Drop dough by kitchen teaspoons, two inches apart, onto prepared cookie sheets.

- Bake 10–13 minutes or until just set and golden at edges. Transfer cookies to wire racks and cool completely.

Baker's Note: To crush the banana chips, place in a small zippered plastic bag. Cover bag with dishtowel and pound with a meat mallet, rolling pin, or soup can.

Makes 28 cookies.

Toasted Coconut Chocolate Chippers

A tropical twist on good old-fashioned chocolate-chip cookies is only minutes away with a hot oven, a cookie sheet, and a few basic pantry items. Toasting the coconut is well worth the minimal effort: it brings out the rich, full flavor of the coconut, transforming these chippers into five-star treats.

1¼ cups shredded coconut
1   18-ounce roll refrigerated chocolate-chip cookie dough
1   teaspoon coconut (or rum) extract (optional)

- Preheat oven to 350°. Evenly spread coconut onto ungreased cookie sheet.

- Toast coconut 9–12 minutes or until golden brown; remove from oven and cool completely on sheet.

- Spray cookie sheets with nonstick cooking spray. Break up cookie dough into large bowl; let stand 10–15 minutes to soften. Add the cooled toasted coconut and coconut or rum extract, if desired; mix well with your fingers, the paddle attachment of an electric stand mixer, or a wooden spoon.

- Spray cookie sheets with nonstick cooking spray. Drop dough by kitchen teaspoons, two inches apart, onto prepared cookie sheets.

- Bake 10–13 minutes or until just set and golden at edges. Transfer cookies to wire racks and cool completely.

Makes 28 cookies.

Drop Cookies

Mint Chocolate Chippers

A batch of chocolate-chip cookies still warm from the oven is reason enough for celebration. But if you add a dose of peppermint to the cookies and accompany them with several mugfuls of hot chocolate, you have a full-fledged party.

1 18-ounce roll refrigerated chocolate-chip cookie dough
1¼ teaspoons peppermint extract

Preheat oven to 350°. Spray cookie sheets with nonstick cooking spray.

Break up cookie dough into large bowl; let stand 10–15 minutes to soften. Add the peppermint extract; mix well with your fingers, the paddle attachment of an electric stand mixer, or a wooden spoon.

Drop dough by kitchen teaspoons, two inches apart, onto prepared cookie sheets.

Bake 10–13 minutes or until just set and golden at edges. Transfer cookies to wire racks and cool completely.

Makes 24 cookies.

Kona Coconut & Coffee Cookies

Basic sugar cookie dough becomes something altogether extraordinary when blended with espresso, coconut, and nuts. Baked to a perfect golden brown, these cookies have the power to transport you to a Hawaiian paradise in just a few nibbles.

1   18-ounce roll refrigerated sugar cookie dough
1   tablespoon instant coffee (or espresso) powder
2   teaspoons rum (or vanilla) extract
1   8-ounce package cream cheese, softened
1   7-ounce package shredded coconut
1   cup sliced, lightly toasted almonds, cooled (optional)

• Preheat oven to 350°. Spray cookie sheets with nonstick cooking spray.

• Break up cookie dough into large bowl; let stand 10–15 minutes to soften.

• In a small cup dissolve coffee powder in the extract. Add coffee mixture, cream cheese, coconut, and nuts, if desired, to cookie dough; mix well with your fingers, the paddle attachment of an electric stand mixer, or a wooden spoon.

• Drop dough by kitchen teaspoons, two inches apart, onto prepared cookie sheets.

• Bake 10–13 minutes or until just set and golden at edges. Remove from oven and cool on sheets for 2 minutes; transfer to wire racks and cool completely.

Makes 40 cookies.

Drop Cookies

Peanut Buttery Chocolate Chip-Loaded Cowboy Cookies

If you crave a simple, sturdy cookie, free of pretension and full of homey goodness, here you are. The cookie may sound new-fangled, but the taste is entirely old-fashioned. Loaded with so many good things, you almost need an excuse not to make these cookies.

1	18-ounce roll refrigerated chocolate-chip cookie dough
¾	cup shredded coconut
¾	cup creamy-style peanut butter
½	cup quick or old-fashioned oats
¾	cup chopped roasted peanuts

• Preheat oven to 350°. Spray cookie sheets with nonstick cooking spray.

• Break up cookie dough into large bowl; let stand 10–15 minutes to soften. Add coconut, peanut butter, oats, and peanuts to the cookie dough; mix well with your fingers, the paddle attachment of an electric stand mixer, or a wooden spoon.

• Drop dough by kitchen teaspoons, two inches apart, onto prepared cookie sheets.

• Bake 10–13 minutes or until just set and golden at edges. Transfer cookies to wire racks and cool completely.

Makes 40 cookies.

Almond Joyful Cookies

This outstanding milk chocolate–coconut cookie is extremely simple to make and especially wonderful to eat. The finished product strongly resembles a delicious candy bar of a similar name.

1	18-ounce roll refrigerated sugar cookie dough
¾	cup shredded coconut
1	cup milk chocolate chips
¾	cup whole almonds, coarsely chopped

Preheat oven to 350°. Spray cookie sheets with nonstick cooking spray.

Break up cookie dough into large bowl; let stand 10–15 minutes to soften. Add coconut, milk chocolate chips, and almonds; mix well with your fingers, the paddle attachment of an electric stand mixer, or a wooden spoon.

Drop dough by kitchen teaspoons, two inches apart, onto prepared cookie sheets.

Bake 10–13 minutes or until just set and golden at edges. Transfer cookies to wire racks and cool completely.

Bakers Note: Sliced or slivered almonds, coarsely chopped, may be substituted for the whole chopped almonds.

Makes 32 cookies.

Brown Sugar Pecan Date Drops

I am a full-fledged brown sugar fiend. As a child I was notorious for eating it straight out of the box. These days I have (a modicum) more self-restraint—except perhaps when it comes to these cookies. Chopped dates, brown sugar, pecans, and vanilla create a perfect coalescence of crisp-chewy, brown sugar-y goodness that is unmatched.

1	18-ounce roll refrigerated sugar cookie dough
3	tablespoons packed brown sugar
1	cup chopped pitted dates
⅔	cup chopped lightly toasted pecans (or walnuts), cooled
1	teaspoon vanilla extract

Preheat oven to 350°. Spray cookie sheets with nonstick cooking spray.

Break up cookie dough into large bowl; let stand 10–15 minutes to soften. Add brown sugar, dates, nuts, and vanilla; mix well with your fingers, the paddle attachment of an electric stand mixer, or a wooden spoon.

Drop dough by kitchen teaspoons, two inches apart, onto prepared cookie sheets.

Bake 10–13 minutes or until just set and golden at edges. Transfer cookies to wire racks and cool completely.

Makes 30 cookies.

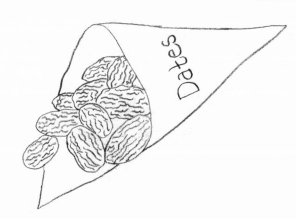

Dates

Lemon-Thyme Sugar Cookies

Part of the fun of making cookies is sharing them and showing off a little. You may be mistaken for a pastry chef when you present these elegant cookies, yet they could not be easier to make. They are just the thing for an afternoon pick-me-up alongside a cup of coffee or tea.

1   18-ounce roll refrigerated sugar cookie dough

1   cup finely chopped lightly toasted walnuts (or almonds), cooled

1   tablespoon chopped thyme leaves or 1½ teaspoons dried thyme

1   tablespoon grated lemon zest

1   recipe Lemon Icing, see page 204

Preheat oven to 350°. Spray cookie sheets with nonstick cooking spray.

Break up cookie dough into large bowl; let stand 10–15 minutes to soften. Add nuts, thyme, and lemon zest; mix well with your fingers, the paddle attachment of an electric stand mixer, or a wooden spoon.

Drop dough by kitchen teaspoons, two inches apart, onto prepared cookie sheets.

Bake 10–13 minutes or until just set and golden at edges. Transfer cookies to wire racks and cool completely. Drizzle cooled cookies with Lemon Icing.

Makes 28 cookies.

Frosted Orange Blossoms

Enhanced with orange zest and a swipe of orange frosting, these delicate citrus cookies are bursting with flavor. The addition of ground coriander lends a distinctive flavor reminiscent of Northern European baked goods. Serve them during the winter holidays as a festive addition to any cookie platter. They are right at home, year-round, as part of an everyday tea ritual, too.

1	18-ounce roll refrigerated sugar cookie dough
1	tablespoons grated orange zest
1	teaspoon ground coriander (or nutmeg)
1	recipe Orange Icing, see page 204

- Preheat oven to 350°. Spray cookie sheets with nonstick cooking spray.

- Break up cookie dough into large bowl; let stand 10–15 minutes to soften. Add orange zest and coriander; mix well with your fingers, the paddle attachment of an electric stand mixer, or a wooden spoon.

- Drop dough by kitchen teaspoons, two inches apart, onto prepared cookie sheets.

- Bake 10–13 minutes or until just set and golden at edges. Transfer cookies to wire racks and cool completely. Spread cooled cookies with Orange Icing.

Baker's Note: For a fanciful presentation, garnish each frosted cookie with a few strips of candied orange zest. For a simpler enhancement, sprinkle with colored decorating sugars.

Makes 24 cookies.

Thanksgiving Cranberry White Chocolate Jumbles

Don't be fooled by the name—these cookies are appealing at any time of the year. The mildly spiced dough is a fine foil for plump, sweet cranberries. They are arguably the perfect bag-lunch cookie and are destined to be the first to disappear from the holiday cookie tray.

1	18-ounce roll refrigerated sugar cookie dough
1	cup white chocolate chips
¾	cup dried cranberries
½	cup sliced almonds, coarsely chopped
1	tablespoon grated orange zest
1	teaspoon pumpkin pie spice (or ground cinnamon)

Preheat oven to 350°. Spray cookie sheets with nonstick cooking spray.

Break up cookie dough into large bowl; let stand 10–15 minutes to soften. Add white chocolate chips, cranberries, almonds, orange zest, and spice; mix well with your fingers, the paddle attachment of an electric stand mixer, or a wooden spoon.

Drop dough by kitchen teaspoons, two inches apart, onto prepared cookie sheets.

Bake 10–13 minutes or until just set and golden at edges. Transfer cookies to wire racks and cool completely.

Makes 30 cookies.

Drop Cookies

Browned Butter–Frosted Cashew Cookies

The short list of ingredients here belies the unique goodness of this simple drop cookie. It is far more than the sum of its parts and is sure to dazzle die-hard dessert-aholics. The nutty-sweet flavor of browned butter—butter you melt until it turns a light caramel hue—is made for cashews.

1   18-ounce roll refrigerated sugar cookie dough
1   cup coarsely chopped roasted, lightly salted cashews
2   tablespoons dark brown sugar
1   recipe Browned Butter Frosting, see page 212

Preheat oven to 350°. Spray cookie sheets with nonstick cooking spray.

Break up cookie dough into large bowl; let stand 10–15 minutes to soften. Add cashews and brown sugar; mix well with your fingers, the paddle attachment of an electric stand mixer, or a wooden spoon.

Drop dough by kitchen teaspoons, two inches apart, onto prepared cookie sheets.

Bake 10–13 minutes or until just set and golden at edges. Transfer cookies to wire racks.

While cookies bake, prepare Browned Butter Frosting. Immediately spoon about one teaspoon icing over each warm cookie. If icing becomes too thick, reheat over low heat. Cool cookies completely.

Makes 28 cookies.

Texas-Size Toffee Scotchie Cookies

These abundantly stuffed beauties are a butterscotch lover's dream come true. Be sure to bake just a few at a time on each sheet—they bake up big, hence the eponymous "Texas-size."

1	18-ounce roll refrigerated sugar cookie dough
⅓	cup firmly packed brown sugar
1½	teaspoons vanilla extract
½	cup old-fashioned or quick oats
1	cup butterscotch chips
2	1.4-ounce milk chocolate covered toffee candy bars, chopped

Preheat oven to 350°. Spray cookie sheets with nonstick cooking spray.

Break up cookie dough into large bowl; let stand 10–15 minutes to soften. Add brown sugar, vanilla, oats, butterscotch chips, and chopped candy bars; mix well with your fingers, the paddle attachment of an electric stand mixer, or a wooden spoon.

Drop dough by rounded one-fourth cupfuls, two inches apart, onto prepared cookie sheets.

Bake 15–18 minutes or until cookies are slightly puffed and edges are golden brown. Cool for 1 minute. Transfer to wire racks and cool completely.

Baker's Note: To make regular-size cookies, prepare cookies as directed above but drop cookies by tablespoons onto prepared cookie sheets. Bake 10–13 minutes or until just set and golden at edges. Transfer cookies to wire racks. Makes about 30 cookies.

Makes 10 big cookies.

Drop Cookies

Coffee & Cream White Chocolate Chunkers

Coffee-enriched and loaded with white chocolate chips, these luxurious cookies are reminiscent of a perfectly rendered cup of cappuccino. For a bit of crunch, try adding a handful of chopped almonds or hazelnuts.

1   **18-ounce roll refrigerated sugar cookie dough**
1   **3-ounce package cream cheese, cut into bits**
1   **teaspoon vanilla extract**
2½ **teaspoons instant espresso (or coffee) powder**
1   **6-ounce white chocolate baking bar, coarsely chopped**
       (or 1 cup white chocolate chips)

- Preheat oven to 350°. Spray cookie sheets with nonstick cooking spray.

- Break up cookie dough into large bowl; add cream cheese to bowl and let stand 10–15 minutes to soften.

- In a small cup combine the vanilla and espresso powder. Add vanilla mixture and white chocolate to the cookie dough and cream cheese bowl; mix well with your fingers, the paddle attachment of an electric stand mixer, or a wooden spoon.

- Drop dough by kitchen teaspoons, two inches apart, onto prepared cookie sheets.

- Bake 10–13 minutes or until just set and golden at edges. Transfer cookies to wire racks.

Makes 28 cookies.

Chocolate-Chip Cream Cheese Softies

My mother used to make a cookie just like this one every Christmas. This version takes about a quarter of the time and effort but yields the same delicious results.

1 18-ounce roll refrigerated chocolate-chip cookie dough
1 8-ounce package cream cheese, cut into bits

- Preheat oven to 350°. Spray cookie sheets with nonstick cooking spray.

- Break up cookie dough into large bowl; add cream cheese bits to bowl and let stand 10–15 minutes to soften.

- Mix dough and cream well with your fingers, the paddle attachment of an electric stand mixer, or a wooden spoon.

- Drop dough by kitchen teaspoons, two inches apart, onto prepared cookie sheets.

- Bake 10–13 minutes or until just set and golden at edges. Transfer cookies to wire racks.

Baker's Note: For a delicious accent, add 1 tablespoon grated orange or lemon zest to the dough.

Makes 40 cookies.

Drop Cookies

Ultimate Almond Cookies

Rich, classic sugar cookie dough, enriched with both almonds and almond extract, makes for simple, and simply wonderful, cookies for almond lovers.

1   18-ounce roll refrigerated sugar cookie dough

1   3-ounce package cream cheese, cut into bits

1   teaspoon almond extract

1¼ cups whole almonds, lightly toasted, cooled and coarsely chopped

1   recipe Almond Icing, see page 205, (optional)

Preheat oven to 350°. Spray cookie sheets with nonstick cooking spray.

Break up cookie dough into large bowl; add cream cheese to bowl and let stand 10–15 minutes to soften.

Add almond extract and almonds to the cookie dough and cream cheese bowl; mix well with your fingers, the paddle attachment of an electric stand mixer, or a wooden spoon.

Drop dough by kitchen teaspoons, two inches apart, onto prepared cookie sheets.

Bake 10–13 minutes or until just set and golden at edges. Transfer cookies to wire racks. If desired, drizzle with Almond Icing.

Makes 30 cookies.

Peanut Brittle Cookies

My husband claims that his maternal grandmother makes the very best versions of several southern classics, including, but not limited to, pecan pie, candied sweet potatoes, and peanut brittle. The latter inspired me to develop this finger-licking, lickity-split cookie. If you want to add a subtle hint of chocolate to this already delicious cookie, replace the toffee baking bits with finely chopped chocolate-covered toffee candy bars.

1	18-ounce roll refrigerated sugar cookie dough
⅔	cup toffee baking bits
1	cup very coarsely chopped salted, dry roasted peanuts

- Preheat oven to 350°. Spray cookie sheets with nonstick cooking spray.

- Break up cookie dough into large bowl; let stand 10–15 minutes to soften. Add the toffee bits and peanuts; mix well with your fingers, the paddle attachment of an electric stand mixer, or a wooden spoon.

- Drop dough by kitchen teaspoons, two inches apart, onto prepared cookie sheets.

- Bake 10–13 minutes or until just set and golden at edges. Transfer cookies to wire racks.

Makes 30 cookies.

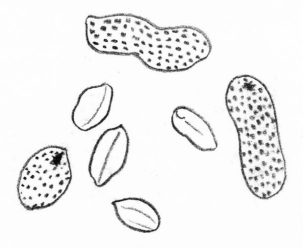

Drop Cookies

Lady Baltimore Cookies

This recipe is inspired by a traditional Southern white cake of the same name. According to one story, the cake was first baked by Alicia Rhett Mayberry of Charleston, South Carolina, for novelist Owen Wister. Wister was supposedly so smitten by the cake, he described it in his next book and even named the novel Lady Baltimore, *published in 1906. The icing, loaded with fruits, nuts, and a splash of spirits, is the secret to this cookie's unique appeal.*

1 18-ounce roll refrigerated sugar cookie dough
1 3-ounce package cream cheese, cut into bits
1 cup chopped pecans, preferably lightly toasted
1 teaspoon almond extract
1 recipe Lady Baltimore Frosting, see page 210

Preheat oven to 350°. Spray cookie sheets with nonstick cooking spray.

Break up cookie dough into large bowl. Add the cream cheese to the bowl; let stand 10–15 minutes to soften.

Add pecans and almond extract to bowl with dough and cream cheese; mix well with your fingers, the paddle attachment of an electric stand mixer, or a wooden spoon.

Drop dough by kitchen teaspoons, two inches apart, onto prepared cookie sheets.

Bake 10–13 minutes or until just set and golden at edges. Transfer cookies to wire racks and cool completely. Generously frost each cookie with a heaping tablespoon of the icing.

Baker's Note: You can substitute the nuts of your choice—almonds, walnuts, hazelnuts—in place of pecans.

Makes 36 cookies.

Peanut Butter Scotchies

In my book, few things are as comforting, reassuring, and just plain delicious as the flavor of butterscotch. Add a hefty dollop of creamy peanut butter and you've got an irresistible homespun treat. Delicious anytime, these cookies are especially excellent dunked in a cold glass of milk in the middle of the afternoon or as a late-night snack.

1	18-ounce roll refrigerated sugar cookie dough
½	cup creamy-style peanut butter
3	tablespoons packed dark brown sugar
1½	teaspoons vanilla extract
1¼	cups butterscotch morsels

Preheat oven to 350°. Spray cookie sheets with nonstick cooking spray.

Break up cookie dough into large bowl; let stand 10–15 minutes to soften. Add the peanut butter, brown sugar, vanilla, and butterscotch morsels; mix well with your fingers, the paddle attachment of an electric stand mixer, or a wooden spoon.

Drop dough by kitchen teaspoons, two inches apart, onto prepared cookie sheets.

Bake 10–13 minutes or until just set and golden at edges. Transfer cookies to wire racks and cool completely.

Makes 32 cookies.

Cherry Rum Drops

Buttery, chewy and fruity—I find the taste and texture of these cookies especially appealing. Equally appreciated during winter holidays and summer picnics, they are as easy to make as they are to eat.

1	18-ounce roll refrigerated sugar cookie dough
½	cup finely chopped maraschino cherries, well-drained
½	cup finely chopped raisins
1	recipe Butter-Rum Icing, see page 210

Preheat oven to 350°. Spray cookie sheets with nonstick cooking spray.

Break up cookie dough into large bowl; let stand 10–15 minutes to soften.

Meanwhile, place chopped cherries between double sheets of paper towels; gently press out excess liquid. Add cherries and raisins to dough; mix well with your fingers, the paddle attachment of an electric stand mixer, or a wooden spoon.

Drop dough by kitchen teaspoons, two inches apart, onto prepared cookie sheets.

Bake 10–13 minutes or until just set and golden at edges. Transfer cookies to wire racks and cool completely. Frost or drizzle with Butter-Rum Icing.

Makes 28 cookies.

Double Lemon Ginger Gems

Ginger and lemon lovers, take note—this is destined to become your favorite cookie, bar none. It is also the perfect summer cookie—simple to make and simply delicious.

1   18-ounce roll refrigerated sugar cookie dough
1   8-ounce package cream cheese, cut into bits
½   cup finely chopped crystallized/candied ginger
2   teaspoons ground ginger
2   teaspoons lemon zest
1   recipe Lemon Icing, see page 204

Preheat oven to 350°. Spray cookie sheets with nonstick cooking spray.

Break up cookie dough into large bowl; add cream cheese bits to bowl and let stand 10–15 minutes to soften.

Add chopped crystallized ginger, ground ginger, and lemon zest; mix well with your fingers, the paddle attachment of an electric stand mixer, or a wooden spoon.

Drop dough by kitchen teaspoons, two inches apart, onto prepared cookie sheets.

Bake 10–13 minutes or until just set and golden at edges. Transfer cookies to wire racks and cool completely. Drizzle with Lemon Icing.

Baker's Note: Lime zest or orange zest may be substituted in place of the lemon zest. Prepare the icing using lime or orange juice in place of the lemon juice.

Makes 42 cookies.

Drop Cookies

Cardamom Currant Tea Cookies

A smidgen of cardamom gives these refined cookies a unique flavor reminiscent of Scandinavian breads and pastries. The dried currants and cardamom create a sweet and spicy balance, but you may, if you wish, substitute ground nutmeg for the cardamom. If you have the time and inclination, soak the currants in sweet cooking wine, such as sherry or Marsala (just enough to cover), for about 30 minutes to plump up the fruit. Drain thoroughly, pat dry with paper towels, and proceed as directed.

1   18-ounce roll refrigerated sugar cookie dough
1   cup dried currants
1   teaspoon ground cardamom (or ground nutmeg)

Preheat oven to 350°. Spray cookie sheets with nonstick cooking spray.

Break up cookie dough into large bowl; let stand 10–15 minutes to soften. Add the currants and cardamom; mix well with your fingers, the paddle attachment of an electric stand mixer, or a wooden spoon.

Drop dough by kitchen teaspoons, two inches apart, onto prepared cookie sheets.

Bake 10–13 minutes or until just set and golden at edges. Transfer cookies to wire racks and cool completely.

Makes 28 cookies.

Spicy Double-Ginger Chocolate Chippers

When Ruth Wakefield added some chopped chocolate to her favorite butter cookie recipe back in the 1930s, she undoubtedly had no idea that she was stirring up the start of a national sensation. More than seventy years later, American affection for chocolate-chip cookies is stronger than ever. This version is spicy and robust thanks to a double dose of ginger and a dash of pepper.

1	18-ounce roll refrigerated chocolate-chip cookie dough
½	cup finely chopped crystallized/candied ginger
1½	teaspoons ground ginger
¼	teaspoon cracked black pepper (optional)

- Preheat oven to 350°. Spray cookie sheets with nonstick cooking spray.

- Break up cookie dough into large bowl; let stand 10–15 minutes to soften. Add crystallized ginger, ground ginger, and pepper, if desired; mix well with your fingers, the paddle attachment of an electric stand mixer, or a wooden spoon.

- Drop dough by kitchen teaspoons, two inches apart, onto prepared cookie sheets.

- Bake 10–13 minutes or until just set and golden at edges. Transfer cookies to wire racks and cool completely.

Makes 28 cookies.

Drop Cookies

2 Formed & Fancy-Shaped Cookies

Formed and fancy-shaped cookies encompass an enticing assortment of delectables, including, but not limited to, hand-shaped classics (such as snickerdoodles), biscotti (twice-baked crunchy cookies, perfect with coffee), madeleines (formed and baked in a shell-shaped tin), and rolled cut-outs.

Formed cookies require more steps than drop cookies, but because these cookies start with premade dough, the effort is still minimal (leaving you plenty of time and energy to concentrate on devouring the cookies). A common denominator of the cookies in this chapter is chilling. With the exception of the biscotti and madeleines, the dough for the cookies in this chapter needs a brief stint in the refrigerator before shaping. The chilling changes the dough's texture, allowing the flavors to meld and making it easier to shape.

In some of this chapter's recipes no extra ingredients are stirred into the dough. Hence so long as the roll of cookie dough is already well-chilled, the cookies will come together in minutes. But if you are making one of the recipes with cookie dough stir-ins, plan on some chilling time. The nice part about this is it gives you some "chilling" time as well so that you take a break, tidy the kitchen a bit, or leave the dough for later that day or the following day.

Basic Rolled Sugar Cookies

These cookies are so easy to make you'll have plenty of time to decorate them to suit your fancy. Whether it's a tasty cream cheese frosting or an assortment of candy trims, you will have a great time letting loose your creative and culinary whims.

1   **18-ounce roll refrigerated sugar cookie dough, well chilled**
    Flour for dusting rolling pin and rolling surface
    Assorted cookie cutters
    Frosting or decorations of your choice (see Chapter 6
        for ideas)

- Preheat oven to 350°. Spray cookie sheets with nonstick cooking spray.

- Cut dough in half crosswise. Refrigerate one half of the dough. On a lightly floured surface, roll out the other half of dough to ⅛-inch thickness.

- Cut out cookies. Place half an inch apart on cookie sheets. Repeat with remaining dough, rerolling as needed.

- Bake 4–6 minutes for small cutter shapes and 7–12 minutes for medium to large cutter shapes. Transfer cookies to wire racks and cool completely.

> Baker's Note: For thicker cookie cut-outs, follow directions above but roll dough to ¼-inch thickness. Bake 5–8 minutes for small cutter shapes and 9–14 minutes for medium to large cutter shapes.

Makes about 36 small to medium-size cookie cut-outs.

Madeleines

Part cake, part cookie, madeleines get their shell shape from madeleine pans, which come in both large and small sizes. Look for pans with a nonstick finish for easy removal. If you want to gild the lily, dip the cooled madeleines in melted chocolate.

1	18-ounce roll refrigerated sugar cookie dough
1	8-ounce package cream cheese, cut into small bits
2	large eggs
1	tablespoon finely chopped lemon zest
1	teaspoon vanilla extract
1	cup sifted powdered sugar

Preheat oven to 350°. Position oven rack to highest position in oven. Spray madeleine pan with nonstick cooking spray.

Break up cookie dough into large bowl; add cream cheese and let stand 10–15 minutes to soften. Add the eggs, lemon zest, and vanilla. Mix with an electric mixer until well blended and smooth.

Spoon the batter into prepared madeleine molds, filling about two-thirds full.

Bake on highest oven rack for 6–7 minutes for small madeleine molds, 8–9 minutes for large madeleine molds, or until the edges are golden and centers are puffed. Turn the madeleines out onto wire racks and cool completely.

Sift cooled madeleines with powdered sugar.

Baker's Note: If you decide to dip the madeleines in melted chocolate (see page 201), dip the plain side (as opposed to the shell side) for a pretty finish.

Makes 28 large or 42 small madeleines.

Formed & Fancy-Shaped Cookies

Chocolate-Kissed Cookies

Who doesn't want to be "kissed" by chocolate? These pretty little cookies are familiar to holiday cookie jars everywhere. Here they are made extra easy with a short list of three ingredients. If the kids are handy, recruit them to help with the rolling of the cookie dough and the placing of the chocolate kisses. Be warned, though: you may need to keep close guard over the chocolates, or else buy an extra bag.

⅓ cup sugar
1 18-ounce roll refrigerated sugar cookie dough, well chilled
24 milk chocolate "kiss" candies, unwrapped

- Preheat oven to 350°. Spray cookie sheets with nonstick cooking spray.

- Place sugar in a shallow dish.

- Cut cookie dough into 12 equal slices. Cut each slice in half. Roll each piece into a ball; roll balls in sugar. Place balls two inches apart on cookie sheets.

- Bake 10–13 minutes or until golden at edges.

- Remove cookie sheet from oven and immediately top each cookie with 1 milk chocolate candy, pressing down firmly so cookie cracks around edges. Transfer cookies to wire racks and cool completely.

Makes 24 cookies.

Decadent Chocolate-Dipped Toffee Chippers

You can stop with the addition of the toffee bits to the cookie dough and you will still have a delectable cookie. But if you give the cookies a dunk in melted chocolate and sprinkle with extra toffee you will have cookies that live up to their name.

- 1 18-ounce roll refrigerated chocolate-chip cookie dough
- 1½ cups toffee baking bits, divided
- 1 recipe Chocolate Drizzle or Dip, see page 201

Break up cookie dough into large bowl; let stand 10–15 minutes to soften. Add ½ cup of the toffee bits; mix well with wooden spoon or fingers. Chill 1 hour in refrigerator or 20–25 minutes in freezer.

Preheat oven to 350°. Spray cookie sheets with nonstick cooking spray.

Shape dough into 28 walnut-size balls. Space two inches apart on prepared cookie sheets; flatten slightly using the bottom of a drinking glass.

Bake 11–13 minutes or until light golden brown at edges. Cool 2 minutes on cookie sheets. Transfer cookies to wire racks and cool completely.

Cover cookie sheet with waxed paper or foil; spray with nonstick cooking spray.

Prepare chocolate dip. Dip one half of each cookie in chocolate; generously sprinkle with remaining 1 cup toffee bits. Place cookies on prepared sheet. Place sheet in refrigerator 30 minutes to set chocolate. Store in refrigerator.

Makes 28 cookies.

Apple Cobbler Cookies

Reminiscent of apple crisp or streusel-topped apple pie, these apple-packed treats are made for autumn eating. They are equally delicious warm or cold, so you can bake a batch to enjoy with a cup of cocoa on the weekend and savor the rest during the week.

1	18-ounce roll refrigerated sugar cookie dough
1	cup peeled, finely chopped tart green apple (about 1 large)
½	cup chopped pecans
1¾	teaspoons cinnamon, divided
¼	cup packed brown sugar
⅓	cup quick-cooking oats
2	tablespoons (¼ stick) butter, melted

- Break up cookie dough into large bowl; let stand 10–15 minutes to soften. Add apple, pecans, and 1 teaspoon cinnamon; mix well with your fingers, the paddle attachment of an electric mixer, or a wooden spoon.

- Chill dough 1 hour in refrigerator or 20–25 minutes in freezer.

- Preheat oven to 350°. Spray cookie sheets with nonstick cooking spray.

- In a small bowl combine the brown sugar, oats, remaining ¾ teaspoon cinnamon, and butter. Roll dough into 1-inch balls. Roll each ball in crumb mixture until well coated. Place cookies on prepared cookie sheets.

- Bake 10–13 minutes or until cookie is firm to the touch and crumb mixture begins to brown. Transfer to wire racks and cool completely.

Makes 32 cookies.

Snickerdoodles

Like a good book, a broken-in pair of slippers, or an old easy chair, snickerdoodles are a sure bet for finding instant calm. So when you want to strike a comforting note—for yourself or someone special—this is your cookie.

⅓ **cup sugar**
2 **teaspoons ground cinnamon**
1 **teaspoon ground nutmeg**
1 **18-ounce roll refrigerated sugar cookie dough, well chilled**

• Preheat oven to 350°. Spray cookie sheets with nonstick cooking spray.

• Combine sugar, cinnamon, and nutmeg in small bowl.

• Cut cookie dough into 12 equal slices. Cut each slice in half. Roll each piece into a ball; roll balls in sugar mixture. Place balls two inches apart on cookie sheets.

• Bake for 10–13 minutes or until edges are golden and centers are just set. Cool on cookie sheets for 2 minutes. Transfer cookies to wire racks and cool completely.

Makes 24 cookies.

Dutch Spice Cookies

Rich with spices, these cookies are wonderful any time of year. However, you're likely to enjoy them most when the temperature dips and the air turns crisp. The combination of dark brown sugar and spices transforms the basic sugar cookie dough, resulting in a cookie evocative of European bakeries.

1   18-ounce roll refrigerated sugar cookie dough
¼   cup packed dark brown sugar
2½ teaspoons ground cinnamon
1   teaspoon ground nutmeg
½   teaspoon ground ginger
¼   teaspoon ground cloves
¼   cup sugar

- Break up cookie dough into large bowl; let stand 10–15 minutes to soften. Add brown sugar, cinnamon, nutmeg, ginger, and cloves; mix well with your fingers, the paddle attachment of an electric mixer, or a wooden spoon.

- Chill dough 1 hour in refrigerator or 20–25 minutes in freezer.

- Preheat oven to 350°. Spray cookie sheets with nonstick cooking spray.

- Place sugar in small flat dish. Roll the dough into 1-inch balls and roll in the sugar.

- Place balls about two inches apart on prepared cookie sheets. Flatten with the bottom of a drinking glass.

- Bake 8–10 minutes or until light brown on bottom. Transfer cookies to wire racks and cool completely.

Makes about 32 cookies.

Mocha Chip Meltaways

Good taste, in every sense, does not come any easier than with these charming little mouthfuls. No one will guess the secret ingredient—peanut butter. Before the cookies are stored or frozen, they can be coated lightly again in powdered sugar to keep them from sticking to one another.

1	tablespoon instant espresso (or coffee) powder
1	teaspoon vanilla extract
1	18-ounce roll refrigerated chocolate-chip cookie dough
¾	cup creamy-style peanut butter
3	tablespoons unsweetened cocoa powder
1½	cups sifted powdered sugar

- In a small dish combine espresso powder and vanilla; stir until dissolved.

- Break up cookie dough into large bowl; let stand 10–15 minutes to soften. Add peanut butter, cocoa powder, and vanilla mixture to cookie dough; mix with hands or wooden spoon to combine.

- Chill dough 1 hour in refrigerator or 20–25 minutes in freezer.

- Preheat oven to 350°. Spray cookie sheets with nonstick cooking spray. Shape dough into 1-inch balls and arrange about two inches apart on prepared cookie sheets.

- Bake 10–12 minutes or until just set. Cool on cookie sheets for 2 minutes.

- Meanwhile, place the powdered sugar in a small bowl. Roll warm cookies, a few at a time, in the powdered sugar, coating them well and transferring them as coated to racks to cool completely.

Makes 40 cookies.

Formed & Fancy-Shaped Cookies

Quick Caramel-Pecan Turtle Cookies

My abiding affection for turtle candies—caramel-pecan clusters covered in milk chocolate—can be traced to my childhood spending habits. On more than one occasion I blew my entire allowance on a bag full of turtles alone. The combination of flavors inspired me to create these cookies, which are child's play to make and to eat.

1   18-ounce roll refrigerated chocolate-chip cookie dough, well chilled
32   chewy chocolate-coated caramel candies, unwrapped
32   pecan halves, preferably lightly toasted, cooled

Preheat oven to 350°. Spray cookie sheets with nonstick cooking spray.

Cut cookie dough into 16 equal slices. Cut each slice in half. Roll each piece into a ball. Place balls two inches apart on ungreased cookie sheets. Flatten slightly with your palm or the bottom of a glass.

Bake 7–10 minutes or until golden at edges. Remove from oven and immediately press one candy into the top of each cookie. Cool 2 minutes on cookie sheets. Remove from cookie sheets; place on wire racks and cool 2–3 minutes.

With knife, spread softened candy on each cookie to cover; top with a pecan half. Cool completely.

Makes 32 cookies.

Formed & Fancy-Shaped Cookies

Sesame Ginger Cookies

One of my most cherished childhood memories is spending Sunday afternoons in San Francisco's Golden Gate Park. My family invariably ended the weekend excursion sipping tea and nibbling cookies at the park's Japanese tea gardens. This ginger-spiked sesame cookie strongly resembles a delicate tea cookie that always appeared in the tea garden's assorted offerings.

1	18-ounce roll refrigerated sugar cookie dough
2	teaspoons ground ginger
1	teaspoon almond extract
½	cup sesame seeds

Break up cookie dough into large bowl; let stand 10–15 minutes to soften. Add the ginger and almond extract; mix well with your fingers, the paddle attachment of an electric stand mixer, or a wooden spoon. Chill dough 1 hour in refrigerator or 25 minutes in freezer.

Preheat oven to 350°. Spray cookie sheets with nonstick cooking spray.

Spread sesame seeds in a small, flat dish. Shape dough into 1-inch balls and roll in sesame seeds to coat. Place balls onto prepared sheets. Gently flatten (slightly) with the bottom of a drinking glass.

Bake 9–12 minutes or until golden brown at edges. Cool 2 minutes; transfer to wire racks and cool completely.

Makes 32 cookies.

Gran's Chocolate-Covered Cherry Cookies

No holiday could pass without my gran receiving multiple boxes of her favorite candy, chocolate-covered cherries, from her children, grandchildren, friends, and admirers. Given her equal affection for cookies, I know she would have loved this twist on her favorite bon-bon. The union of rich chocolate fudge, cherries, and sugar cookie bottoms is irresistible.

- 1 **18-ounce roll refrigerated sugar cookie dough, well chilled**
- 30 **maraschino cherries (about one 10-ounce jar with juice)**
- 1 **cup semisweet chocolate chips**
- ½ **cup canned sweetened condensed milk**

Preheat oven to 350°. Spray cookie sheets with nonstick cooking spray.

Cut cookie dough into 15 equal slices. Cut each slice in half. Roll each piece into a ball. Place balls two inches apart on prepared cookie sheets.

Press down center of each ball with thumb or cork. Drain maraschino cherries, reserving juice. Place a cherry in the center of each cookie.

In a small saucepan combine the chocolate pieces and sweetened condensed milk; cook and stir over low heat until chocolate is melted. Stir in 1 tablespoon of the reserved cherry juice. Spoon about 1 teaspoon of the frosting over each cherry, spreading to cover cherry. (Frosting may be thinned with additional cherry juice, if necessary.)

Bake 9–12 minutes. Transfer cookies to wire racks and cool completely. Cover and store at room temperature up to 2 days.

Makes 30 cookies.

Hazelnut Orange Cookies

Madame Kanyuk, my sister's childhood piano teacher, was as talented in the kitchen as at the keyboard. When it came time for her annual piano recitals, her house was filled with the sweet harmony of both music and baked treats from her native Hungary. I will never forget her hazelnut-orange cookies, a crisp-chewy confection with a generous measure of orange zest and a hint of ground coriander. If you do not have coriander, substitute ground nutmeg or mace.

1	18-ounce roll refrigerated sugar cookie dough
1	cup chopped hazelnuts (or almonds)
2½	teaspoons grated orange peel
½	teaspoon ground coriander (or nutmeg)
⅓	cup granulated sugar
1	recipe Orange Icing, see page 204 (optional)

• Break up cookie dough into large bowl; let stand 10–15 minutes to soften. Add hazelnuts, orange peel, and coriander. Mix well with your fingers, the paddle attachment of an electric mixer, or a wooden spoon.

• Chill dough 1 hour in refrigerator or 20–25 minutes in freezer.

• Preheat oven to 350°. Spray cookie sheets with nonstick cooking spray.

• Place sugar in shallow dish. Roll dough into 1-inch balls; roll in sugar. Arrange balls two inches apart on prepared cookie sheets; flatten to ¼-inch thickness by pressing with the bottom of a drinking glass, dipping the glass into granulated sugar for each round.

• Bake 10–12 minutes or until edges begin to brown. Transfer cookies to wire racks and cool completely. If desired, drizzle with Orange Icing.

Makes about 30 cookies.

Mexican Wedding Cakes

Baked to golden perfection, then dunked in powdered sugar, these melt-in-your-mouth treats won't last more than a few minutes when offered to a crowd. No one will believe they began with a roll of cookie dough.

1	18-ounce roll refrigerated sugar cookie dough
1½	cups whole almonds
¼	cup cornstarch
1¼	teaspoons almond extract
1½	cups sifted powdered sugar

- Break up cookie dough into large bowl; let stand 10–15 minutes to soften.

- Meanwhile, finely chop almonds in a food processor or with sharp kitchen knife.

- Add the almonds, cornstarch, and almond extract to the cookie dough; mix well with your fingers, the paddle attachment of an electric mixer, or a wooden spoon.

- Chill dough 1 hour in refrigerator or 20–25 minutes in freezer.

- Preheat oven to 350°. Spray cookie sheets with nonstick cooking spray. Shape dough into 1-inch balls. Place balls one inch apart on prepared cookie sheets.

- Bake 11–14 minutes or until just golden at edges and centers are set. Cool 2 minutes on cookie sheets.

- Place powdered sugar in small dish. Roll warm balls, one at a time, in powdered sugar to coat. Transfer to wire racks and cool completely.

Makes about 36 cookies.

Jungle Crunch Chocolate-Chip Cookies

The lumpy-bumpy appearance of these cookies comes courtesy of a heaping handful of chopped banana chips, cashews, toffee baking bits, and chocolate chips. They are guaranteed pleasers.

1	18-ounce roll refrigerated chocolate-chip cookie dough
⅔	cup coarsely chopped banana chips
½	cup coarsely chopped lightly salted roasted cashews (or peanuts)
1	cup toffee baking bits

• Break up cookie dough into large bowl; let stand 10–15 minutes to soften. Add banana chips and cashews; mix well with your fingers or a wooden spoon.

• Chill dough 1 hour in refrigerator or 20–25 minutes in freezer.

• Preheat oven to 350°. Spray cookie sheets with nonstick cooking spray.

• Place the toffee bits in a small bowl. Roll dough into 1-inch balls. Roll each ball in toffee bits, pressing gently so that toffee adheres to dough. Place cookies on prepared cookie sheets.

• Bake 10–12 minutes or until just golden at edges. Cool 2 minutes on cookie sheets. Transfer to wire racks and cool completely.

Makes 32 cookies.

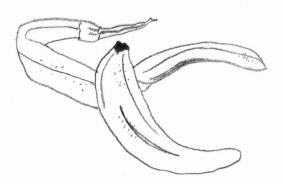

Formed & Fancy-Shaped Cookies

Tuscan Cornmeal Cookies

Cornmeal may seem an unusual cookie ingredient to most Americans, but it is a common dessert ingredient in Northern Italy. This sugar-coated cookie, with its rustic cornmeal crunch and citrus-rosemary infused flavor, is destined to turn questioners into converts. Both hearty and heartwarming, these cookies are not-too-sweet companions to coffee or a terrific finish to any simple pasta dinner.

1   18-ounce roll refrigerated sugar cookie dough
3   tablespoons light brown sugar
⅓   cup yellow or white cornmeal
1   tablespoon chopped fresh rosemary (or 1½ teaspoons dried, crumbled rosemary)
1   tablespoon grated lemon zest
1   teaspoon vanilla extract
1   recipe Lemon Icing, see page 204, (optional)

Break up cookie dough into large bowl; let stand 10–15 minutes to soften. Add the brown sugar, cornmeal, rosemary, lemon zest, and vanilla extract; mix well with your fingers or a wooden spoon.

Chill dough 1 hour in refrigerator or 20–25 minutes in freezer.

Preheat oven to 350°. Spray cookie sheets with nonstick cooking spray.

Shape dough into 1-inch balls; place two inches apart on prepared cookie sheets. Flatten cookies with a fork dipped in sugar.

Bake 10–12 minutes or until golden brown. Cool 2 minutes on cookie sheet. Transfer to wire racks and cool completely. If desired, drizzle with Lemon Icing.

Makes 30 cookies.

Lemon Poppyseed Petites

Poppyseeds are more than decoration in these petite morsels—they have a subtle, slightly earthy, slightly spicy flavor, not to mention a delicate crunch. Their flavor finds perfect complement here with the rich sugar cookie dough and familiar tang of lemon zest.

1   18-ounce roll refrigerated sugar cookie dough
1½ tablespoons poppyseeds
2   teaspoons grated lemon zest
1   cup sifted powdered sugar

• Break up cookie dough into a large bowl; let stand 10–15 minutes to soften. Add the poppyseeds and lemon zest; mix well with your fingers or a wooden spoon.

• Chill dough 1 hour in refrigerator or 20–25 minutes in freezer.

• Preheat oven to 350°. Spray cookie sheets with nonstick cooking spray. Shape dough into 1-inch balls; place two inches apart on prepared cookie sheets.

• Bake 10–12 minutes or until golden brown. Cool 2 minutes on cookie sheets; remove from cookie sheets.

• Place powdered sugar in a plastic bag. While still warm, transfer several cookies at a time to the bag. Gently shake until coated. Transfer cookies to a wire rack to cool. When completely cooled, gently shake cookies again in powdered sugar.

Makes 30 cookies.

Formed & Fancy-Shaped Cookies

Frosted Maple-Nut Minis

"You must try these!" a friend wrote on the card enclosed in a box of frosted maple cookies. She procured the cookies at a newly opened bakery in her hometown, and, knowing my fondness for cookies, brown sugar, and maple, she felt compelled to send some along for sampling. What a friend! This is my version of the mouth-watering cookie.

1	18-ounce roll refrigerated sugar cookie dough
¾	cup creamy-style peanut butter
2	teaspoons maple extract
¼	cup packed brown sugar
¼	teaspoon ground cinnamon
1	recipe Maple Icing, see page 205

Preheat oven to 350°. Spray cookie sheets with nonstick cooking spray.

Break up cookie dough into large bowl; let stand 10–15 minutes to soften. Add the peanut butter, maple extract, brown sugar, and cinnamon; mix well with your fingers or a wooden spoon.

Shape dough into 1-inch balls; place two inches apart on prepared cookie sheets.

Bake 10–12 minutes or until golden brown. Cool 2 minutes on cookie sheets; remove from cookie sheets and cool completely. When cool, frost or drizzle with Maple Icing.

Makes 36 cookies.

Picture-Perfect Chocolate-Peanut Pinwheels

1	18-ounce roll refrigerated sugar cookie dough, well chilled
¼	cup all-purpose flour
¼	cup unsweetened cocoa powder
1	cup miniature semisweet chocolate chips
1	cup finely chopped roasted, lightly salted peanuts

•Break up half of cookie dough into large bowl; let stand 10–15 minutes to soften. Add flour to the cookie dough; mix well with your fingers, the paddle attachment of an electric stand mixer, or a wooden spoon.

•Add cocoa powder to second half of cookie dough; mix well with your fingers, the paddle attachment of an electric stand mixer, or a wooden spoon.

•Roll out each dough half between pieces of waxed paper to form a 12 x 6-inch rectangle. Remove the top pieces of waxed paper; sprinkle chocolate chips and half of the peanuts over sugar cookie dough rectangle; gently press into dough. Top with cocoa dough half; press down gently to seal. Remove top piece of waxed paper. Roll up tightly, from long end of dough.

•Sprinkle remaining peanuts onto a piece of waxed paper; roll dough log in peanuts, gently pressing to coat. Wrap dough log in waxed paper or plastic wrap. Chill at least 1 hour until firm.

•Preheat oven to 375°. Lightly spray a cookie sheet with nonstick cooking spray.

•With a sharp knife, cut dough into ¼-inch slices. Place slices two inches apart on prepared sheet. Bake 8–10 minutes or until edges are firm to the touch. Transfer cookies to wire racks and cool completely.

Makes about 36 cookies.

Formed & Fancy-Shaped Cookies

Stained Glass Cookie Cut-Outs

Looking for a cookie that is a first-prize winner in looks as well as taste? These stained glass cookies look as though made by an expert, but even the youngest of children can help make them. I give directions below for punching a hole in the cookies, so that they may be hung in the window or on a tree as ornaments. This step is not necessary if the only plan is to eat the cookies. Use one color per "pane" or sprinkle two or three different colors of crushed candy in each "pane" for a kaleidoscope effect. Just make sure to crush the candies fine to ensure even melting.

- 12 pieces (about 2 ounces) clear hard fruit candies, unwrapped
- 1 18-ounce roll refrigerated sugar cookie dough, well chilled
- ¼ cup all-purpose flour
- Assorted decorations: icing, frosting, small candies, melted chocolate (see Chapter 6 for decorating ideas)
- 6 to 8 yards of ribbon (optional)

Preheat oven to 350°. Line cookie sheets with parchment paper or foil. (If using foil, smooth out all wrinkles.) Place 3 to 4 candies of the same color in small plastic bag; seal bag. With hammer or flat side of meat mallet, gently pound to crush candy. Repeat with remaining candies, using several different colors.

Cut chilled dough in half: wrap and refrigerate one-half until needed. Remove wrapper from remaining half roll; coat sides of dough with 2 tablespoons of the flour. Roll out dough to ⅛-inch thickness, using additional flour as needed to prevent sticking. Cut out dough with floured 2-inch cookie cutter. With smaller cookie cutter or sharp knife, cut out center of cookie, leaving about ½-inch frame.

- Place small center cutouts on separate cookie sheet sprayed with non-stick cooking spray. Bake 4–6 minutes or until light golden brown.

- Brush excess flour from cut-out cookies. With spatula, place cut-out shapes two inches apart on paper-lined cookie sheets. With drinking straw, make hole in top of each cookie. Place $\frac{1}{2}$ teaspoon crushed candy in center ("pane") of each cut-out cookie, making sure candy touches edges of cookie. (Do not mound candy in centers of cookies.)

- Bake 5–9 minutes or until edges of cookies are light golden brown and candy is melted and fills center of cookie. Cool 5 minutes on cookie sheets or until candy is hardened. Reshape holes for ribbon, if necessary. Remove cookies from cookie sheets. Cool completely. Repeat with remaining half of dough and candy.

- Frost and decorate cookies. Cut ribbon into 9- to 12-inch lengths. Insert piece of ribbon through hole of each cookie; tie in knot or bow.

Makes 36 cookies.

Formed & Fancy-Shaped Cookies

Stained Glass Cookie Cut-Outs

Cookie Pops for Cookie Bouquets

A bouquet of flowers is always lovely, but a "bouquet" of delicious, decorated cookies is all the sweeter. Consider delivering your gift in a vase, bundled with pretty ribbon, or placed in a box surrounded by pastel tissue paper. This is also a great activity for children's birthday parties. Bake the cookies ahead of time then have the children decorate their individual "bouquets" with an assortment of colored frostings, sprinkles, and candies for a memorable and delectable take-away gift.

1   18-ounce roll refrigerated sugar cookie dough (or chocolate-chip cookie dough), well chilled

8   long, flat wooden craft sticks

Assorted decorations: icing, frosting, small candies, melted chocolate (see Chapter 6 for decorating ideas)

- Preheat oven to 375°. Spray cookie sheets with nonstick cooking spray.

- Slice cookie dough into 8 equal pieces; roll each slice into a ball. Place 4 balls at a time onto prepared cookie sheet, spacing far apart.

- Insert wooden sticks into each ball to resemble a lollipop; flatten dough to ½-inch thickness with the bottom of a drinking glass.

- Bake 13–15 minutes or until edges are golden and centers are just set. Cool on cookie sheet for 1 minute. Remove to wire racks and cool completely.

- Decorate as desired.

Baker's Note: Wooden craft sticks can be found at craft stores. To make a bouquet, bundle cookies together and tie colorful ribbons around sticks. For easier handling, place sticks in a vase or in a box.

Makes 8 cookies for 1 cookie bouquet.

One Big Party Cookie

You need only be a kid at heart to enjoy a party devoted to decorating—and eating— these giant cookies. Place some of the icings in ketchup-style squirt bottles (available at craft and kitchen stores) to allow for abstract impressionism or precision lettering and drawing. For a great potluck party, bake multiple giant cookies (one per guest), prepare the icings ahead of time and have guests bring their favorite candies for decorating.

1 **18-ounce roll refrigerated sugar cookie dough (or chocolate-chip cookie dough), well chilled**
Assorted decorations: icing, frosting, small candies, melted chocolate (see Chapter 6 for decorating ideas)

- Preheat oven to 350°. Line a cookie sheet or a 12- or 14-inch pizza pan with aluminum foil; spray foil with nonstick cooking spray.

- Slice dough into ¼-inch-thick slices. With floured fingers, press slices evenly into the prepared pan or cookie sheet, pressing edges together to form one large circle.

- Bake 15–18 minutes or until edges are golden and center is just barely set.

- Remove from oven and place pan on top of wire rack. Cool completely on pan. Decorate with frosting and candies as desired.

Makes 12 to 14 servings.

Formed & Fancy-Shaped Cookies

Cookie Dominoes

Who says you can't play with your food? These whimsical cookies are at once both charming and child's play.

1 18-ounce roll refrigerated sugar cookie dough, well chilled
½ cup semisweet chocolate chips

• Preheat oven to 350°. Spray cookie sheets with nonstick cooking spray.

• Cut dough in half lengthwise; refrigerate one half. On a lightly floured surface, roll out dough to ¼-inch thickness to form a 10 x 6-inch rectangle. Cut into 10 equal-size rectangles.

• Place rectangles two inches apart on cookie sheet. With a sharp knife, score each rectangle in half, crosswise. Gently press morsels, point side down, into dough to form domino numbers. Repeat with remaining dough.

• Bake 8–11 minutes or until edges are golden. Cool on cookie sheets for 1 minute. Transfer to wire racks and cool completely.

Baker's Note: To score each cookie in half, cut approximately one-third to halfway through the dough, being careful not to cut all the way through.

Makes 20 cookies.

Big Bunny Cookie

Be sure to include this at your next Easter gathering. Bake the big cookie ahead of time and have the kids decorate, if you like. To make decorating this fun and yummy cookie extra easy, place the different decorations and candies in each cup of a muffin tin.

1   18-ounce roll refrigerator sugar cookie dough, well chilled
1   cup canned strawberry or other pink cake frosting
¾   cup shredded coconut
    Assorted small candies

- Preheat oven to 350°. Line a cookie sheet with aluminum foil; spray foil with nonstick cooking spray.

- Cut the cookie roll crosswise into thirds. On the bottom half of the lined sheet, pat 1 portion into a 6-inch circle to form the bunny's head.

- Position the remaining 2 portions of dough atop head, and pat into two 8-inch-long bunny ears, connecting the ears to the bunny head.

- Bake 13–16 minutes or until edges are golden and center is just barely set.

- Carefully transfer bunny cookie to a flat surface or wire rack by lifting foil from cookie sheet. Cool completely before decorating.

- Spread frosting over bunny to within 1 inch of edges; sprinkle with coconut. Use candies to decorate bunny's face as desired.

Makes 12 to 14 servings.

Formed & Fancy-Shaped Cookies

Chocolate Peppermint Cookie Hearts

It may seem calculated, but the fact is that planning for love in a modern world is essential. Your calculations are destined to add up if you make someone who matters a plate of these whimsical heart cookies.

1   **18-ounce roll refrigerated sugar cookie dough**
2   **tablespoons unsweetened cocoa**
1   **recipe Dark Chocolate Frosting, see page 211**
$\frac{1}{8}$ **teaspoon peppermint extract**
$\frac{1}{2}$ **cup coarsely crushed peppermint candies or candy canes**

Break up cookie dough into large bowl; let stand 10–15 minutes to soften. Add cocoa; mix with wooden spoon or fingers until well blended. Chill 1 hour in refrigerator or 20–25 minutes in freezer.

Preheat oven to 350°. Spray cookie sheets with nonstick cooking spray.

On lightly floured surface, roll out half of the dough at a time to $\frac{1}{4}$-inch thickness. With $2\frac{1}{2}$-inch heart-shaped cookie cutter, cut out cookies. Place $\frac{1}{2}$-inch apart on prepared cookie sheets. Repeat with remaining dough, rerolling as needed.

Bake 10–12 minutes or until golden at edges and just set. Remove cookies from cookie sheets; place on wire racks. Cool completely.

Prepare Dark Chocolate Frosting, stirring in the peppermint extract. Spread about 2 teaspoons icing onto each cookie. Sprinkle each with crushed candies.

Makes 30 cookies.

Easy Roll & Go Sliced Cookies

Edged in chopped nuts, toffee bits, candies or coloring sugar, these easy roll-slice-and-bake cookies are a fast fix for dressing up sugar cookies.

1   18-ounce roll refrigerated sugar cookie dough (or chocolate-chip cookie dough), well chilled

1   cup of any of the following: finely chopped nuts (any variety), toffee bits, colored sugar, or small decorator candies

Preheat oven to 350°. Spray cookie sheets with nonstick cooking spray. Place chopped nuts or candies on a large plate; gently shake plate to distribute evenly.

Carefully remove wrapper from sugar cookie dough, keeping log of dough intact. Immediately roll dough in chopped nuts or candy, gently pressing dough into bits. Transfer dough to a cutting board and slice into 24 even slices. Space slices two inches apart on prepared cookie sheets.

Bake cookies 10–12 minutes or until golden at edges; cool on sheets 1 minute. Transfer cookies to wire racks and cool completely.

Makes 24 cookies.

Formed & Fancy-Shaped Cookies

Walnut Raisin Biscotti

1   18-ounce roll refrigerated sugar cookie dough
⅔   cup all-purpose flour
1   cup chopped walnuts, lightly toasted, cooled
1   cup coarsely chopped raisins
2   teaspoons vanilla extract

Preheat oven to 350°. Lightly spray a cookie sheet with nonstick cooking spray.

Break up cookie dough into large bowl; let stand 10–15 minutes to soften. Add the flour, walnuts, raisins, and vanilla extract to the cookie dough; mix well with your fingers, the paddle attachment of an electric stand mixer, or a wooden spoon.

Divide dough into two equal halves. On the cookie sheet, shape each dough half into a 12-inch-long, 2-inch-wide, ¾-inch-high rectangle, spacing the dough halves about three inches apart.

Bake 26–28 minutes or until the logs are deep golden brown and spring back in the center when touched. Remove sheet from oven; keep oven on.

Using two pancake turners, lift logs, one at a time, from the cookie sheet to a cutting board. Using a sharp knife, cut one of the logs into ¾-inch-wide slices. *Note: for longer biscotti, cut at a deep diagonal; for shorter biscotti, cut log crosswise.* Repeat with second log. Place slices on the same cookie sheet (do not worry about the spacing).

•Bake slices 5 minutes; remove from oven and turn over all of the slices. Return cookie sheet to oven and bake 5 minutes longer. Remove sheet from oven and immediately transfer biscotti to a wire rack; cool completely.

Baker's Note: For half batches of biscotti, follow all of the directions above but halve the ingredients. Make one biscotti log instead of two and proceed as directed above. Wrap and freeze the second half of dough for a future batch of biscotti or cookies.

Makes 28 biscotti.

Formed & Fancy-Shaped Cookies

Walnut Raisin Biscotti

Lemon Pistachio Biscotti

1   18-ounce roll refrigerated sugar cookie dough
⅔   cup all-purpose flour
1½ cups shelled, roasted pistachios
1   tablespoon grated lemon zest
1   teaspoon vanilla extract
1   recipe Lemon Icing, see page 204, (optional)

- Preheat oven to 350°. Lightly spray a cookie sheet with nonstick cooking spray.

- Break up cookie dough into large bowl; let stand 10–15 minutes to soften. Add flour, pistachios, lemon zest, and vanilla extract to the cookie dough; mix well with your fingers, the paddle attachment of an electric stand mixer, or a wooden spoon.

- Divide dough into two equal halves. On the cookie sheet, shape each dough half into a 12-inch-long, 2-inch-wide, ¾-inch-high rectangle, spacing the dough halves about three inches apart.

- Bake 26–28 minutes or until the logs are deep golden brown and spring back in the center when touched. Remove sheet from oven; keep oven on.

- Using two pancake turners, lift logs, one at a time, from the cookie sheet to a cutting board. Using a sharp knife, cut one of the logs into ¾-inch-wide slices. *Note: for longer biscotti, cut at a deep diagonal; for shorter biscotti, cut log crosswise.* Repeat with second log. Place slices on the same cookie sheet (do not worry about the spacing).

- Bake slices 5 minutes; remove from oven and turn over all of the slices. Return cookie sheet to oven and bake 5 minutes longer. Remove sheet from oven and immediately transfer biscotti to a wire rack; cool completely. If desired, drizzle one side of each biscotti with Lemon Icing.

Makes 28 biscotti.

Milk Chocolate Cherry Biscotti

- 1   18-ounce roll refrigerated sugar cookie dough
- ⅔   cup all-purpose flour
- ¾   cup coarsely chopped dried cherries (or dried cranberries)
- ¾   cup milk chocolate chips
- 1   teaspoon pure almond extract

- Preheat oven to 350°. Lightly spray a cookie sheet with nonstick cooking spray.

- Break up cookie dough into large bowl; let stand 10–15 minutes to soften. Add the flour, dried fruit, milk chocolate chips, and almond extract to the cookie dough; mix well with your fingers, the paddle attachment of an electric stand mixer, or a wooden spoon.

- Divide dough into two equal halves. On the cookie sheet, shape each dough half into a 12-inch-long, 2-inch-wide, ¾-inch-high rectangle, spacing the dough halves about three inches apart.

- Bake 26–28 minutes or until the logs are deep golden brown and spring back in the center when touched. Remove sheet from oven; keep oven on.

- Using two pancake turners, lift logs, one at a time, from the cookie sheet to a cutting board. Using a sharp knife, cut one of the logs into ¾-inch-wide slices. *Note: for longer biscotti, cut at a deep diagonal; for shorter biscotti, cut log crosswise.* Repeat with second log. Place slices on the same cookie sheet (do not worry about the spacing).

- Bake slices 5 minutes; remove from oven and turn over all of the slices. Return cookie sheet to oven and bake 5 minutes longer. Remove sheet from oven and immediately transfer biscotti to a wire rack; cool completely.

Makes 28 biscotti.

Formed & Fancy-Shaped Cookies

Quaresimale (Loaded Almond Biscotti)

1   18-ounce roll refrigerated sugar cookie dough
⅔ cup all-purpose flour
1½ cups whole almonds, lightly toasted, cooled, very
       coarsely chopped
1¼ teaspoons pure almond extract
1   teaspoon ground cinnamon

Preheat oven to 350°. Lightly spray a cookie sheet with nonstick cooking spray.

Break up cookie dough into large bowl; let stand 10–15 minutes to soften. Add the flour, almonds, almond extract, and cinnamon to the cookie dough; mix well with your fingers, the paddle attachment of an electric stand mixer, or a wooden spoon.

Divide dough into two equal halves. On the cookie sheet, shape each dough half into a 12-inch-long, 2-inch-wide, ¾-inch-high rectangle, spacing the dough halves about three inches apart.

Bake 26–28 minutes until the logs are deep golden brown and spring back in the center when touched. Remove sheet from oven; keep oven on.

Using two pancake turners, lift logs, one at a time, from the cookie sheet to a cutting board. Using a very sharp knife, cut one of the logs into ¾-inch-wide slices. *Note: for longer biscotti, cut at a deep diagonal; for shorter biscotti, cut log crosswise.* Repeat with second log. Place slices on the same cookie sheet; do not worry about the spacing.

Bake slices 5 minutes; remove from oven and turn over all of the slices. Return cookie sheet to oven and bake 5 minutes longer. Remove sheet from oven and immediately transfer biscotti to a wire rack; cool completely.

Makes 28 biscotti.

Cranberry Eggnog Biscotti

1   18-ounce roll refrigerated sugar cookie dough
⅔   cup all-purpose flour
1½ cups dried cranberries, coarsely chopped
1   tablespoon grated orange zest
1   teaspoon ground cinnamon
1   teaspoon ground nutmeg
1   teaspoon vanilla extract

- Preheat oven to 350°. Lightly spray a cookie sheet with nonstick cooking spray.

- Break up cookie dough into large bowl; let stand 10–15 minutes to soften. Add flour, cranberries, orange zest, cinnamon, nutmeg, and vanilla extract to the cookie dough; mix well with your fingers, the paddle attachment of an electric stand mixer, or a wooden spoon.

- Divide dough into two equal halves. On the cookie sheet, shape each dough half into a 12-inch-long, 2-inch-wide, ¾-inch-high rectangle, spacing the dough halves about three inches apart.

- Bake 26–28 minutes or until the logs are deep golden brown and spring back in the center when touched. Remove sheet from oven; keep oven on.

- Using two pancake turners, lift logs, one at a time, from the cookie sheet to a cutting board. Using a sharp knife, cut one of the logs into ¾-inch-wide slices. *Note: for longer biscotti, cut at a deep diagonal; for shorter biscotti, cut log crosswise.* Repeat with second log. Place slices on the same cookie sheet; (do not worry about the spacing).

- Bake slices 5 minutes; remove from oven and turn over all of the slices. Return cookie sheet to oven and bake 5 minutes longer. Remove sheet from oven and immediately transfer biscotti to a wire rack; cool completely.

Makes 28 biscotti.

Formed & Fancy-Shaped Cookies

Chocolate-Dipped Pecan Praline Biscotti

1 18-ounce roll refrigerated sugar cookie dough
⅔ cup all-purpose flour
1 cup chopped pecans, lightly toasted, cooled
1 cup English toffee baking bits
1 teaspoon vanilla extract
1 recipe Chocolate Dip or Drizzle, see page 201, (optional)

•Preheat oven to 350°. Lightly spray a cookie sheet with nonstick cooking spray.

•Break up cookie dough into large bowl; let stand 10–15 minutes to soften. Add flour, pecans, toffee bits, and vanilla extract to the cookie dough; mix well with your fingers, the paddle attachment of an electric stand mixer, or a wooden spoon.

•Divide dough into two equal halves. On the cookie sheet, shape each dough half into a 12-inch-long, 2-inch-wide, ¾-inch-high rectangle, spacing the dough halves about three inches apart.

•Bake 26–28 minutes until the logs are deep golden brown and spring back in the center when touched. Remove sheet from oven; keep oven on.

•Using two pancake turners, lift logs, one at a time, from the cookie sheet to a cutting board. Using a sharp knife, cut one of the logs into ¾-inch-wide slices. *Note: for longer biscotti, cut at a deep diagonal; for shorter biscotti, cut log crosswise.* Repeat with second log. Place slices on the same cookie sheet (do not worry about the spacing).

•Bake slices 5 minutes; remove from oven and turn over all of the slices. Return cookie sheet to oven and bake 5 minutes longer. Remove sheet from oven and immediately transfer biscotti to a wire rack; cool completely. If desired, dip one end of each biscotti in 1 recipe of the Chocolate Dip; place on wax paper–lined cookie sheet and refrigerate until chocolate is firm.

Makes 28 biscotti.

Ginger Lime Biscotti

1	18-ounce roll refrigerated sugar cookie dough
⅔	cup all-purpose flour
1	cup finely chopped candied ginger
2	teaspoons ground ginger
1	tablespoon grated lime zest
1	teaspoon vanilla extract
1	recipe Lime Icing, see page 204 (optional)

Preheat oven to 350°. Lightly spray a cookie sheet with nonstick cooking spray.

Break up cookie dough into large bowl; let stand 10–15 minutes to soften. Add the flour, candied ginger, ground ginger, lime zest, and vanilla extract to the cookie dough; mix well with your fingers, the paddle attachment of an electric stand mixer, or a wooden spoon.

Divide dough into two equal halves. On the cookie sheet, shape each dough half into a 12-inch-long, 2-inch-wide, ¾-inch-high rectangle, spacing the dough halves about three inches apart.

Bake 26–28 minutes or until the logs are deep golden brown and spring back in the center when touched. Remove sheet from oven; keep oven on.

Using two pancake turners, lift logs, one at a time, from the cookie sheet to a cutting board. Using a sharp knife, cut one of the logs into ¾-inch-wide slices. *Note: for longer biscotti, cut at a deep diagonal; for shorter biscotti, cut log crosswise.* Repeat with second log. Place slices on the same cookie sheet; do not worry about the spacing.

Bake slices 5 minutes; remove from oven and turn over all of the slices. Return cookie sheet to oven and bake 5 minutes longer. Remove sheet from oven and immediately transfer biscotti to a wire rack; cool completely. If desired, drizzle each biscotti with Lime Icing.

Makes 28 biscotti.

Formed & Fancy-Shaped Cookies

Mocha White Chocolate Chunk Biscotti

1   18-ounce roll refrigerated sugar cookie dough
1   tablespoon instant espresso (or coffee) powder
1   teaspoon vanilla extract
½   cup all-purpose flour
2   tablespoons unsweetened cocoa powder
1   6-ounce white chocolate baking bar, chopped into chunks

Preheat oven to 350°. Lightly spray a cookie sheet with nonstick cooking spray.

Break up cookie dough into large bowl; let stand 10–15 minutes to soften. In a small cup combine espresso powder and vanilla. Add vanilla mixture, flour, cocoa powder, and white chocolate chunks to the cookie dough; mix well with your fingers, the paddle attachment of an electric stand mixer, or a wooden spoon.

Divide dough into two equal halves. On the cookie sheet, shape each dough half into a 12-inch-long, 2-inch-wide, ¾-inch-high rectangle, spacing the dough halves about three inches apart.

Bake 26–28 minutes until the logs are deep golden brown and spring back in the center when touched. Remove sheet from oven; keep oven on.

Using two pancake turners, lift logs, one at a time, from the cookie sheet to a cutting board. Using a sharp knife, cut one of the logs into ¾-inch-wide slices. *Note: for longer biscotti, cut at a deep diagonal; for shorter biscotti, cut log crosswise.* Repeat with second log. Place slices on the same cookie sheet; do not worry about the spacing.

•Bake slices 5 minutes; remove from oven and turn over all of the slices. Return cookie sheet to oven and bake 5 minutes longer. Remove sheet from oven and immediately transfer biscotti to a wire rack; cool completely.

Baker's Note: For half batches of biscotti, follow all of the directions above but halve the ingredients. Make one biscotti log instead of two and proceed as directed above. Wrap and freeze the second half of dough for a future batch of biscotti or cookies.

Makes 28 biscotti.

Formed & Fancy-Shaped Cookies

Mocha White Chocolate Chunk Biscotti

3 Bar Cookies

Think of the most decadent cookie ever to pass your palate. Chances are it was a bar cookie. Silky cheesecake squares, lemon bars, cookie dough–filled brownies, pecan pie bars, coffeehouse carmelitas—bar cookies are magical in the world of home baking, able to highlight any flavor combination, please any appetite, and match any occasion. What's more, bar cookies typically come together in a flash and dirty but one pan.

Many of the recipes in this chapter follow one straightforward template: press the refrigerated cookie dough in a pan, sprinkle, spread or pour a delicious topping over all, and bake. Sometimes chopped nuts are pressed into the cookie dough layer, powdered sugar is sifted over the bars, or a rich layer of silky frosting is spread over all for a delicious adornment.

Other cookies in this chapter are as simple as stirring in a few tasty additions to the refrigerated cookie dough, pressing the dough into a pan, and baking until golden. Once the cookies are cool, cut into bars, squares, or diamond shapes.

Caramel Chocolate Pecan Bars

I have long loved the flavors of caramel, chocolate, and pecans, especially in combination. These easy bars satisfy my sweet cravings, without fuss, when my sweet tooth strikes.

1   18-ounce roll refrigerated sugar cookie dough, well chilled
1⅓ cups caramel apple dip (or caramel ice cream topping)
3   tablespoons all-purpose flour
2   cups chopped pecans
1⅓ cups semisweet chocolate chips

Preheat oven to 350°. Spray a 13 x 9-inch pan with nonstick cooking spray or line with foil.

Cut cookie dough into ¼-inch-thick slices. Arrange slices in bottom of the prepared pan. With floured fingers, press dough evenly to form crust.

Bake 10–14 minutes or until light golden brown (dough will appear slightly puffed).

While crust bakes, combine caramel topping and flour in a small bowl; blend until smooth.

Remove pan from oven. Immediately sprinkle partially baked crust with pecans and chocolate chips. Drizzle with caramel mixture.

Return to oven; bake an additional 13–17 minutes or until topping is bubbly. Remove from oven and cool completely. Cut into bars.

Makes 36 bars.

Double Peanut Butter Chocolate-Chip Bars

Pinched for time? Whip up a batch of these bars, which taste every bit as delicious and decadent as they sound.

- 1   18-ounce roll refrigerated sugar cookie dough, well chilled
- 2   cups milk or semisweet chocolate chips
- 1   14-ounce can sweetened condensed milk
- 1½ cups lightly salted roasted peanuts
- 1   10-ounce package peanut butter–flavored baking chips
- 1   recipe Peanut Butter Icing, see page 207

- Preheat oven to 350°. Spray a 15 x 10 x 1-inch baking pan with non-stick cooking spray or line with foil.

- Cut cookie dough into ⅛-inch-thick slices. Arrange slices in bottom of the prepared pan. With floured fingers, press dough evenly to form crust.

- Evenly sprinkle dough with chocolate chips; drizzle condensed milk evenly over chips. Sprinkle peanuts and peanut butter baking chips evenly over condensed milk layer. Gently press down with back of spoon or spatula.

- Bake 24–27 minutes or until edges are set and firm to the touch. Cool completely in pan. Drizzle with Peanut Butter Icing. Let icing set before cutting into bars.

Makes 64 bars.

Coconut Cashew Apricot Bars

A short list of yummy ingredients is all it takes for these wickedly delicious bars. The flavor far surpasses the time it will take you to make them.

1 18-ounce roll refrigerated sugar cookie dough, well chilled
1 14-ounce can sweetened condensed milk
1½ cups chopped dried apricots
¾ cup butterscotch chips
1⅓ cups shredded coconut
1½ cups chopped lightly salted cashews

Preheat oven to 350°. Spray a 15 x 10 x 1-inch baking pan with non-stick cooking spray or line with foil.

Cut cookie dough into ⅛-inch-thick slices. Arrange slices in bottom of the prepared pan. With floured fingers, press dough evenly to form crust.

Drizzle condensed milk over dough, spreading evenly. Sprinkle with apricots, butterscotch chips, coconut, and cashews. Press down firmly with back of spoon or spatula.

Bake 20–23 minutes or until golden brown. Cool completely in pan.

Makes 64 bars.

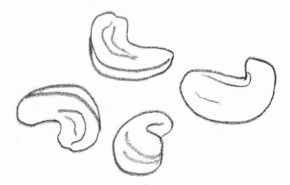

Italian Panforte Petites

These dainty cookies capture the flavor of panforte, a dense Italian confection similar to American fruitcake. Cut the baked bars into bite-sized pieces.

1   **18-ounce roll refrigerated sugar cookie dough**
1   **10- to 12-ounce can unsalted mixed nuts, coarsely chopped**
⅔   **cup butterscotch baking chips**
⅔   **cup mixed dried fruit bits (or chopped dried fruit of choice)**
½   **cup shredded coconut**

Preheat oven to 350°. Spray a 9-inch square baking pan with nonstick cooking spray or line with foil.

Break up cookie dough into large bowl; let stand 10–15 minutes to soften. Add nuts, butterscotch chips, and dried fruit to dough; mix well with your fingers, the paddle attachment of an electric stand mixer, or a wooden spoon. With floured hands press dough into the prepared pan. Sprinkle coconut over top of dough; gently press into dough.

Bake 27–30 minutes or until a toothpick inserted near center comes out clean. Cool completely in pan on wire rack. Cut into small squares.

Makes 32 squares.

Colossal Cranberry Pecan Chunkers

Years ago I was stranded in Chicago's O'Hare Airport for most of the day on a Christmas trip home from college. Exhausted and ravenous, I stumbled into a sandwich shop for sustenance and discovered one of the most delectable bar cookies I have ever encountered. Thick, rich, and loaded with dried cranberries, pecans, and white chocolate, I almost wished for an added delay. Here is my shortcut version of that mouth-watering cookie. The vanilla extract is optional, but works wonderfully to bring out the cookie's colossal combination of flavors.

1	18-ounce roll refrigerated sugar cookie dough
1½	cups coarsely chopped pecans
¾	cup dried cranberries
1	teaspoon vanilla extract (optional)
1½	cups white chocolate chips, divided
1	tablespoon vegetable shortening

• Preheat oven to 350°. Spray a 9-inch square baking pan with nonstick cooking spray or line with foil.

• Break up cookie dough into large bowl; let stand 10–15 minutes to soften. Add pecans, cranberries, vanilla, if desired, and 1 cup white chocolate chips; mix well (mixture will be stiff). With floured hands, press dough into the prepared pan.

• Bake 27–30 minutes or until a toothpick inserted near center comes out clean. Cool completely in pan on wire rack.

• In a small saucepan set over low heat melt reserved ½ cup white chocolate chips and shortening, stirring constantly until smooth; drizzle over cooled base. Cut into squares.

Baker's Note: For an extra-rich variation, frost the bars with White Chocolate Cream Cheese Frosting (see page 214) in place of the white chocolate drizzle.

Makes 16 chunky squares.

Peanut Brittle Bars

Peanut brittle lovers, mark your calendars: January 26th is National Peanut Brittle Day. One taste of these bars—bolstered with both toffee bits and butterscotch chips—and you won't be able to stop celebrating.

1	18-ounce roll refrigerated sugar cookie dough, well chilled
2	cups lightly salted, roasted peanuts
1	cup butterscotch chips
½	cup toffee baking bits
1	12½-ounce jar caramel ice cream topping
3	tablespoons all-purpose flour

- Preheat oven to 350°. Spray a 15 x 10 x 1-inch baking pan with non-stick cooking spray or line with foil.

- Cut cookie dough into ⅛-inch slices. Arrange slices in bottom of the prepared pan. Using floured fingers, press dough evenly in pan to form crust.

- Bake 8–11 minutes or until light golden brown and slightly puffed.

- Remove pan from oven and sprinkle peanuts, butterscotch chips, and toffee bits over warm base. In a small bowl combine caramel topping and flour; blend well. Drizzle caramel mixture evenly over peanut layer.

- Bake an additional 15–18 minutes or until topping is set and golden brown. Remove from oven and cool completely. Cut into bars.

Baker's Note: Milk or semisweet chocolate chips may be substituted for the butterscotch chips.

Makes 36 bars.

Chubby Rocky Road Bars

Whenever I make these bars they disappear instantly. Consequently, I make them often for sharing at potlucks, picnics, and other pitch-ins.

1	18-ounce roll refrigerated chocolate-chip cookie dough
1	cup semi-sweet chocolate morsels, divided
1½	cups miniature marshmallows
½	cup chopped walnuts (or pecans)

Preheat oven to 350°. Spray an 8- or 9-inch square baking pan with nonstick cooking spray or line with foil.

Break up dough into the prepared pan; with floured fingers, press dough into pan to form an even layer.

Bake 27–30 minutes or until toothpick inserted in center comes out clean. Remove from oven and immediately sprinkle with half of the chocolate chips; keep oven on. Let stand 5 minutes until chips are shiny; with knife, spread chocolate chips to cover cookie layer.

Top with marshmallows, remaining morsels, and walnuts. Press down lightly. Bake an additional 5 minutes or until marshmallows begin to puff.

Remove from oven and cool on wire rack 15–20 minutes. Cut warm bars into pieces with wet knife.

Makes 16 big squares.

Deep Dark Chocolate Truffle Bars

These loaded confections are a luxurious coalescence of a crunchy cookie crust and a liqueur-spiked layer of chocolate fudge. All that and they can be made up to a day ahead of time, too.

1   18-ounce roll refrigerated sugar cookie dough, well chilled
1½ cups semisweet chocolate chips
1   14-ounce can sweetened condensed milk
1½ tablespoons orange (or coffee) liqueur
½   cup white chocolate chips
1   tablespoon shortening

Preheat oven to 350°. Spray a 13 x 9-inch pan with nonstick cooking spray or line with foil. Cut cookie dough into ¼-inch-thick slices. Arrange slices in bottom of the prepared pan. With floured fingers, press dough evenly to form crust.

Bake 15–18 minutes or until deep golden brown (dough will appear puffed). Cool completely.

In medium saucepan over low heat combine semisweet chocolate chips and sweetened condensed milk; cook and stir until smooth and chips are melted. Remove from heat and stir in liqueur; spread over cooled crust.

In small saucepan over low heat, combine white chocolate chips and shortening. Stir until melted and smooth. Drizzle over chocolate-liqueur layer. Refrigerate 1–2 hours or until set. Cut into bars or squares. Store in refrigerator.

Makes 36 pieces.

Bar Cookies

German Chocolate Cake Bars

All of the flavors of German Chocolate Cake—milk chocolate, coconut, and pecans—are loaded into this tasty recipe. It's an ooey-gooey confection for anyone in need of a hearty dose of decadence.

1   18-ounce roll refrigerated chocolate-chip cookie dough, well chilled
2   large eggs
2   teaspoons vanilla extract
1   15-ounce can coconut pecan frosting
1   14-ounce can sweetened condensed milk
1   cup coarsely chopped pecans
1   11½-ounce package milk chocolate chips
2   tablespoons vegetable shortening

•Preheat oven to 350°. Spray a 15 x 10 x 1-inch baking pan with non-stick cooking spray or line with foil.

•Cut cookie dough into ⅛-inch slices. Arrange slices in bottom of the prepared pan. Using floured fingers, press dough evenly in pan to form crust.

•Bake 8–11 minutes or until light golden brown and slightly puffed. Remove pan from oven and cool 5 minutes.

•Meanwhile, in a large bowl beat the eggs with electric beaters until foamy. Add vanilla extract, frosting, and condensed milk; beat 1 minute at medium speed or until well blended. Spoon and spread filling evenly over partially baked crust. Sprinkle with pecans.

•Bake an additional 20–24 minutes or until top is deep golden brown and center is set. Cool 5 minutes.

•In small saucepan combine the chocolate chips and shortening. Cook and stir over medium heat until smooth and chips are melted. Carefully pour over filling; gently spread to cover. Refrigerate 1½ hours or until chocolate is set. Cut into small bars. Store in refrigerator.

Makes 64 bars.

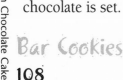

Crispy Caramel Cashew Bars

Can a bar cookie be spectacular? If milk chocolate, caramel, and cashews top your list of favorite flavors, then the answer is a resounding "yes."

1   18-ounce roll refrigerated chocolate-chip cookie dough, well chilled
2   cups milk chocolate chips, divided
1   16-ounce container (about 1½ cups) caramel apple dip, divided
3   cups crisp rice cereal
1¼ cups chopped lightly salted roasted cashews

- Preheat oven to 350°. Spray a 13 x 9-inch pan with nonstick cooking spray or line with foil.

- Slice cookie dough into ¼-inch-thick slices. Arrange slices in bottom of the prepared pan. With floured fingers, press dough evenly to form crust.

- Bake 10–14 minutes or until light golden brown (dough will appear slightly puffed). Remove from oven; cool 15 minutes.

- In large saucepan combine 1 cup of the chocolate chips and 1 cup of the caramel dip. Cook over medium heat until melted and smooth, stirring constantly. Remove from heat. Stir in cereal and cashews; immediately spread over cooled crust.

- In small saucepan, combine remaining 1 cup chips and ½ cup caramel dip. Cook over medium heat until melted and smooth, stirring constantly. Spread over cereal mixture. Refrigerate 30 minutes or until set. Cut into bars.

Baker's Note: Other nuts may be substituted for the cashews. Any other roasted or toasted coarsely chopped nuts will work, or use roasted mixed nuts.

Makes 36 bars.

Bar Cookies

Triple-Decker Chocolate-Chip Peanut Butter Bars

Some occasions call for restraint, others for indulgence. Be sure to serve these bars on the latter type of occasion. Everyone knows how good chocolate and peanut butter are in combination, but this layered bar elevates the duo to new hedonistic heights.

- 1½ cups sifted powdered sugar
- 1½ cups creamy peanut butter
- 1½ teaspoons vanilla extract
- 1 18-ounce roll refrigerated chocolate-chip cookie dough, well chilled

- Preheat oven to 350°. Spray an 8- or 9-inch pan with nonstick cooking spray or line with foil.

- In a medium bowl combine the powdered sugar, peanut butter, and vanilla; mix well with a wooden spoon (mixture will be stiff).

- Cut cookie dough in half. With floured fingers, press half of dough in bottom of the prepared pan. Press peanut butter mixture evenly over dough. Crumble remaining half of cookie dough evenly over peanut butter mixture.

- Bake 27–30 minutes or until golden brown and firm to the touch. Remove from oven and cool completely. Cut into bars.

Makes 16 big bars.

Lipsmacker Lemon Bars

Lemon bars are one of my sentimental favorites. Tart lemon curd on a sugar cookie crust? It's hard to beat, especially with a cup of hot tea and a good book close at hand.

1	18-ounce roll refrigerated sugar cookie dough, well chilled
4	large eggs, slightly beaten
1⅓	cups sugar
¼	cup all-purpose flour
1	teaspoon baking powder
¾	cup lemon juice
⅓	cup sifted powdered sugar

Preheat oven to 350°. Spray a 13 x 9-inch pan with nonstick cooking spray or line with foil. Cut cookie dough into ¼-inch-thick slices. Arrange slices in bottom of the prepared pan. With floured fingers, press dough evenly to form crust.

Bake 10–14 minutes or until light golden brown (dough will appear slightly puffed). Remove from oven.

While crust bakes whisk the eggs, sugar, flour, and baking powder in a large bowl; blend well. Whisk in lemon juice. Pour mixture over warm, partially baked crust.

Return pan to oven and bake 22–25 minutes or until filling is just set. Remove from oven and cool completely. Cut into bars and remove from pan; sprinkle with powdered sugar.

Baker's Note: If you cannot get enough lemon, drizzle or spread cooled bars with 1 recipe Lemon Icing (see page 204) in place of sifting with powdered sugar.

Makes 36 bars.

Bar Cookies

Peanut Butter & Strawberry Jam Bars

These old-fashioned bar cookies combine the best of peanut butter and strawberry jam in one delicious mouthful—comfort food to the max.

1	18-ounce roll refrigerated sugar cookie dough, well chilled
1	14-ounce can sweetened condensed milk
1	cup creamy-style peanut butter
1	teaspoon vanilla extract
3	large egg yolks
⅔	cup strawberry jam or preserves

Preheat oven to 350°. Spray a 13 x 9-inch pan with nonstick cooking spray or line with foil.

Cut cookie dough into ¼-inch-thick slices. Arrange slices in bottom of the prepared pan. With floured fingers, press dough evenly to form crust.

Bake 10–14 minutes or until light golden brown (dough will appear slightly puffed). Remove from oven.

Meanwhile, in a medium bowl combine the sweetened condensed milk, peanut butter, vanilla, and egg yolks; mix until smooth. Spoon and carefully spread milk mixture evenly over crust; dollop with spoonfuls of jam and swirl slightly with the tip of a knife. Return to oven; bake an additional 20–25 minutes or until just set.

Remove from oven and cool completely. Cut into bars.

Makes 36 bars.

Chocolate-Chip Cheesecake Chubbies

I am a fool for cheesecake. Lucky for me with these delectable bars I can get all of the richness and flavor of my favorite dessert with minimal fuss and a fraction of the time it takes to make a regular cheesecake. Be sure to cool the pan of bars completely before cutting into squares.

1	8-ounce package cream cheese, softened
⅓	cup sugar
1	large egg
1	teaspoon vanilla extract
1	cup semisweet chocolate chips
1	18-ounce roll refrigerated chocolate-chip cookie dough

Preheat oven to 350°. Spray an 8- or 9-inch pan with nonstick cooking spray or line with foil.

In a medium bowl combine the cream cheese, sugar, egg, and vanilla; beat with electric beaters on high, stopping to scrape down sides of the bowl with a rubber spatula once or twice, until smooth. Stir in chocolate chips; set aside.

Cut cookie dough in half. With floured fingers, press half of dough in bottom of prepared pan. Spread cream cheese mixture over dough. Crumble and sprinkle remaining half of the cookie dough over cream cheese mixture (need not completely cover cream cheese layer).

Bake 32–36 minutes or until golden brown and firm to the touch; cool completely. Cut into bars. Serve room temperature or chilled. Store in refrigerator.

Makes 16 bars.

Raspberry & White Chocolate Cheesecake Chubbies

My first encounter with raspberry–white chocolate cheesecake was at a bakery located in close proximity to my summer office job. These extravagant bars capture the same exquisite union of flavors in one great big chubby bar.

1	8-ounce package cream cheese, softened
¼	cup sugar
1	large egg
1	teaspoon vanilla extract
1½	cups white chocolate chips, divided
1	18-ounce roll refrigerated sugar cookie dough
⅓	cup seedless raspberry jam or preserves
1	tablespoon vegetable shortening

Preheat oven to 350°. Spray an 8- or 9-inch pan with nonstick cooking spray or line with foil.

In a medium bowl combine cream cheese, sugar, egg, and vanilla; beat with electric beaters on high, stopping to scrape down the sides of the bowl with a rubber spatula once or twice, until smooth. Stir in 1 cup white chocolate chips; set aside.

Cut cookie dough in half. With floured fingers, press half of the dough in bottom of prepared pan. Spread cream cheese mixture over dough; dollop with teaspoons of jam. Crumble and sprinkle remaining half of cookie dough over cream cheese mixture (need not completely cover cream cheese and jam layer).

Bake 32–36 minutes or until golden brown and firm to the touch; cool completely. In small saucepan over low heat, combine remaining ½ cup white chocolate chips and shortening. Stir until melted and smooth. Drizzle over bars. Cut into bars. Serve room temperature or chilled. Store in refrigerator.

Makes 16 bars.

Waikiki White Chocolate Pineapple Bars

Pineapple boosts the flavor of these island-inspired bars. Just be sure to drain the pineapple thoroughly, and pat it dry to keep the crust crisp.

1   18-ounce roll refrigerated sugar cookie dough, well chilled
1   20-ounce can crushed pineapple, drained and patted dry
      between paper towels
1   cup white chocolate chips
1⅓ cups shredded coconut
1   cup coarsely chopped macadamia nuts (or blanched almonds)
1   14-ounce can sweetened condensed milk

Preheat oven to 350°. Spray a 13 x 9-inch pan with nonstick cooking spray or line with foil.

Cut cookie dough into ¼-inch slices. Arrange slices in bottom of prepared baking pan. With floured fingers, press dough evenly in pan to form crust.

Evenly sprinkle pineapple, white chocolate chips, coconut, and nuts over prepared dough. Evenly drizzle with sweetened condensed milk.

Bake 24–27 minutes or until edges are bubbly and center is just lightly browned. Remove from oven and immediately run a narrow metal spatula or table knife around edges of pan to loosen. Cool completely in pan on a wire rack; cut into bars.

Makes 36 bars.

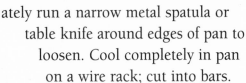

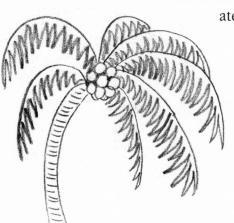

Espresso Chocolate-Chip Cheesecake Bars

Rich and gutsy, and especially delicious when shared with a fellow coffee lover, these bars will deliver you into the lap of luxury in just a few nibbles.

1	18-ounce roll refrigerated chocolate-chip cookie dough, well chilled
2	8-ounce packages cream cheese, softened
½	cup sugar
2	large eggs
4	teaspoons instant espresso (or coffee) powder
2	teaspoons vanilla extract
⅔	cup semisweet miniature chocolate chips

• Preheat oven to 350°. Spray a 13 x 9-inch pan with nonstick cooking spray or line with foil.

• Cut cookie dough into ¼-inch-thick slices. Arrange slices in bottom of the prepared pan. With floured fingers, press dough evenly to form crust.

• Bake 10–13 minutes or until light golden brown (dough will appear slightly puffed). Remove from oven.

• In a medium mixing bowl place the cream cheese, sugar, and eggs; beat on medium speed with an electric mixer until smooth. In a small bowl stir together the instant espresso and vanilla until powder is dissolved. Beat the espresso mixture into cream cheese mixture until combined.

• Spread cream cheese mixture evenly over warm crust; evenly sprinkle with miniature chocolate chips. Bake 19–23 minutes or until just set. Cool in pan on a wire rack; cut into bars and chill. Store in refrigerator.

Makes 36 bars.

Bar Cookies

Becca's Cinnamon Cashew Triangles

I developed this cookie for my sister, who is allergic to peanuts and hazelnuts but loves other nuts, especially cashews. These pretty cookie triangles match her personality—at once both sophisticated and homey.

1	18-ounce roll refrigerated sugar cookie dough, room temperature
¾	cup lightly salted roasted cashews, coarsely chopped
½	cup toffee baking bits
1¼	teaspoons ground cinnamon, divided
⅔	cup sifted powdered sugar
2	to 3 teaspoons milk

Preheat oven to 350°. Spray a 9-inch pan with nonstick cooking spray or line with foil.

Break up cookie dough into large bowl. Let stand 10–15 minutes to soften. Add cashews, toffee baking bits, and 1 teaspoon cinnamon; mix well with your fingers, the paddle attachment of an electric stand mixer, or a wooden spoon. With floured fingers, press dough in bottom of the prepared pan.

Bake 23–27 minutes or until golden brown and toothpick inserted in center comes out clean. Cool 30 minutes.

In small bowl blend the powdered sugar, remaining ¼ teaspoon cinnamon, and enough milk to make drizzling consistency; drizzle over bars. Cool an additional 45 minutes or until completely cooled. Cut into 16 squares; cut each bar in half diagonally to make triangles.

Makes 32 triangles.

Bar Cookies

Elegant Orange Bars with Almond Cookie Crust

I took a batch of these to a graduate school potluck party and the guests inhaled them. Once the crumbs had settled, more than a dozen people asked for the recipe, which I was as happy to share then as I am now. Similar to a traditional lemon bar, the filling is made extra easy with orange juice concentrate. If almonds do not suit your fancy, leave them out or use the nut of your choice—they are delicious any way you choose to serve them.

1	18-ounce roll refrigerated sugar cookie dough, well chilled
⅔	cup chopped almonds
3	tablespoons all-purpose flour
1	6-ounce container frozen orange juice concentrate, thawed
2	teaspoons grated orange zest
2	large eggs
3	to 4 tablespoons sifted powdered sugar (optional)

- Preheat oven to 350°. Spray a 13 x 9-inch pan with nonstick cooking spray or line with foil.

- Cut dough into ¼-inch-thick slices. Arrange slices in bottom of the prepared pan. With floured fingers, press dough evenly to form crust. Sprinkle with almonds; press firmly into dough.

- Bake 10–13 minutes or until dough is golden brown (dough will appear slightly puffed). Remove from oven.

- Meanwhile, in a medium bowl whisk together the orange juice concentrate, orange zest, and eggs; blend until smooth with wire whisk. Carefully pour orange mixture over partially baked crust.

- Bake 18–23 minutes or until edges are golden brown and filling is set. Remove from oven and cool completely. Cut into bars and sprinkle with powdered sugar if desired.

Makes 36 bars.

Raspberry Teatime Triangles

Turn a cup of Earl Grey into a tea party with these elegant raspberry treats. The secret to their success? A crackly brown-sugar layer combined with not-too-sweet raspberry preserves and a scattering of chopped walnuts.

- 1 **18-ounce roll refrigerated sugar cookie dough, room temperature**
- 3 **tablespoons all-purpose flour**
- ¼ **teaspoon salt**
- ¼ **teaspoon baking soda**
- 2 **large eggs**
- ½ **cup firmly packed brown sugar**
- 1 **teaspoon vanilla extract**
- ½ **cup seedless raspberry preserves**
- 1 **cup chopped walnuts (or pecans)**
- ¼ **cup sifted powdered sugar (optional)**

Preheat oven to 350°. Spray a 9-inch square baking pan with nonstick cooking spray or line with foil.

Crumble cookie dough into the prepared pan; press to form one even layer. Bake 12–15 minutes or until deep golden (dough will appear puffed). Cool completely on wire rack.

In a small bowl whisk together the flour, salt, and baking soda. Set aside. In a separate bowl beat together the eggs, brown sugar, and vanilla with whisk until blended. Gradually whisk in the flour mixture just until blended.

Spoon and spread jam evenly over cooled crust. Pour filling on top, then sprinkle evenly with nuts.

Bake 22–25 minutes, until center is completely set and top is golden. Cool in pan on wire rack. Cut into 16 squares, then halve each square diagonally. Sprinkle with powdered sugar, if desired.

Makes 32 triangles.

Bar Cookies

Cranberry Crumble Bars

One bite of these humble, crumble-topped bars can turn my day around. Add a good book and a comfy chair and I'm all set. Sometimes "crumble" bars turn into just that: crumble. But you won't have any problems with this recipe. Sugar cookie dough, mixed with a very short list of stir-ins, makes a sturdy base and topping for the thick layer of tart, whole-berry cranberry sauce. Few recipes are less complicated or more versatile, making these treats suitable for serving year-round.

1   18-ounce roll refrigerated sugar cookie dough, room temperature
1⅓ cups regular or quick-cooking oats
¼   cup firmly packed dark brown sugar
1   16-ounce can whole cranberry sauce
½   cup chopped pecans (or walnuts)

- Preheat oven to 350°. Spray a 9-inch square baking pan with nonstick cooking spray or line with foil.

- Crumble cookie dough into large bowl; add oats and brown sugar. Mix with your fingers or a wooden spoon until combined. Reserve 1 cup of the mixture for topping.

- Press the remaining oat mixture into the bottom of the prepared pan. Bake 17–20 minutes or until light golden brown.

- Carefully spread the cranberry sauce evenly over the partially baked crust. Stir the nuts into the reserved topping; sprinkle over cranberry sauce. Lightly pat topping into cranberry layer.

- Bake 18–21 minutes more or till top is lightly browned. Cool in pan on a wire rack. Cut into bars.

Makes 16 big bars.

Golden Bars

The refreshing flavor of lemon, together with the subtle mingling of walnuts, coconut, and golden raisins, makes for a guaranteed favorite.

1	18-ounce roll refrigerated sugar cookie dough, well chilled
4	large eggs
1	cup packed light brown sugar
2	teaspoons finely shredded lemon peel
1/4	cup lemon juice
1/2	teaspoon salt
1 1/2	cups chopped walnuts (or pecans)
2	cups shredded coconut
1	cup golden raisins

- Preheat oven to 350°. Spray a 13 x 9-inch pan with nonstick cooking spray or line with foil.

- Cut cookie dough into 1/4-inch-thick slices. Arrange slices in bottom of the prepared pan. With floured fingers, press dough evenly to form crust.

- Bake 10–13 minutes or until dough is golden brown (dough will appear slightly puffed). Remove from oven.

- Meanwhile, for filling, in medium bowl beat the eggs, brown sugar, lemon peel, lemon juice, and salt with an electric mixer on medium speed for 2 minutes. Stir in the nuts, coconut, and raisins.

- Pour filling over partially baked crust. Bake 18–21 minutes or until lightly browned around edges and center is set. Cool in pan on a wire rack. Cut into bars.

Makes 36 bars.

Apricot Ambrosia Bars

I have fond memories of my maternal grandmother making her special version of ambrosia, a mesmerizing concoction of vanilla custard, apricots, whipped cream, almonds, and toasted coconut. Just as the name implies, it was heaven. This easy bar lives up to its namesake and is nothing short of a showstopper. It's bound to bring cheers at any gathering.

1	18-ounce roll refrigerated sugar cookie dough, well chilled
2	8-ounce packages cream cheese, softened
⅔	cup granulated sugar
2	large eggs
¾	teaspoon almond extract
¾	cup apricot preserves
1	cup shredded coconut
½	cup sliced almonds

- Preheat oven to 350°. Spray a 13 x 9-inch pan with nonstick cooking spray or line with foil.

- Cut cookie dough into ¼-inch-thick slices. Arrange slices in bottom of the prepared pan. With floured fingers, press dough evenly to form crust.

- Bake 10–13 minutes or until dough is golden brown (dough will appear slightly puffed). Remove from oven.

- Meanwhile, in another bowl beat the cream cheese, granulated sugar, eggs and almond extract with an electric mixer set on high until smooth, stopping mixer occasionally to scrape the sides of the bowl with a rubber spatula.

- Spread over partially baked crust. Dollop preserves over cream cheese layer (does not need to completely cover cream cheese layer). Sprinkle coconut and almonds over preserves. Return to oven and bake 22–25 minutes, until coconut is golden. Cool completely; cut into bars. Serve room temperature or chilled. Store in refrigerator.

Makes 36 bars.

Pumpkin Pie Bars

My brother is something of a dessert purist, especially around the holidays. So when it comes to pumpkin pie, he eschews any "unnecessary" additions, such as cranberries, nuts, or chocolate. He applauds this handheld version of his favorite toothsome treat, in part because of its "pure" pumpkin pie flavor, but also because it is literally easier than pie to prepare. If you don't have pumpkin pie spice blend, substitute 1¾ teaspoons ground cinnamon, ½ teaspoon ground ginger, and ¼ teaspoon ground cloves.

1	18-ounce roll refrigerated sugar cookie dough, well chilled
2	large eggs
1	15-ounce can pure pumpkin
1	5-ounce can (⅔ cup) evaporated milk
½	cup packed brown sugar
2½	teaspoons pumpkin pie spice

Preheat oven to 350°. Spray a 13 x 9-inch pan with nonstick cooking spray or line with foil.

Cut cookie dough into ¼-inch-thick slices. Arrange slices in bottom of the prepared pan. With floured fingers, press dough evenly to form crust.

Bake 10–13 minutes or until dough is golden brown (dough will appear slightly puffed). Remove from oven.

In a medium bowl mix the eggs, pumpkin, evaporated milk, brown sugar, and pumpkin pie spice with wire whisk until smooth. Pour mixture over the partially baked crust.

Bake for 33–37 minutes or until just set. Cool in pan on wire rack. Cut into squares. Store in the refrigerator. Serve room temperature or chilled.

Baker's Note: For a chocolate treat, substitute chocolate-chip cookie dough for sugar cookie dough. Prepare as above except sprinkle pumpkin layer with ½ cup miniature semisweet chocolate chips just before baking.

Makes 24 big squares.

Double Blueberry Squares

This is a "pull out all the stops" pleasure for blueberry lovers. For obvious reasons, leftovers are unlikely.

1	18-ounce roll refrigerated sugar cookie dough, well chilled
⅔	cup quick-cooking rolled oats
3	tablespoons packed brown sugar
1	cup frozen blueberries, thawed
½	cup blueberry preserves
1	teaspoon finely shredded lemon peel

• Preheat oven to 350°. Spray an 8- or 9-inch baking pan with nonstick cooking spray or line with foil.

• Crumble cookie dough into a medium mixing bowl; add oats and brown sugar. Mix with your fingers or a wooden spoon until blended. Reserve 1 cup of the mixture. Press remaining dough mixture into the bottom of the prepared pan.

• Bake for 17–20 minutes or until golden brown. Remove from oven.

• In a medium mixing bowl combine frozen blueberries, preserves, and lemon peel. Carefully spread over partially baked crust. Sprinkle with reserved dough mixture, pressing lightly into blueberry mixture.

• Bake 19–23 minutes more or until top is golden and firm to the touch. Cool completely in pan on a wire rack. Cut into squares.

Makes 16 squares.

Almond Toffee Bars

Who would guess that such a short list of ingredients could lead to such sweet success? It's easy to keep all of the ingredients on hand, too, for spur-of-the-moment splurges. Earmark this one as a sure bet for group gatherings both for its brief preparation requirements and universal appeal.

1   18-ounce roll refrigerated sugar cookie dough, well chilled
1   cup semi-sweet (or milk) chocolate chips
1   cup toffee baking bits
1   cup sliced (or chopped) almonds
1   14-ounce can sweetened condensed milk

Preheat oven to 350°. Spray a 13 x 9-inch pan with nonstick cooking spray or line with foil.

Cut cookie dough into ¼-inch-thick slices. Arrange slices in bottom of the prepared pan. With floured fingers, press dough evenly to form crust.

Sprinkle the chocolate chips, toffee bits, and almonds evenly over prepared crust. Drizzle evenly with sweetened condensed milk.

Bake 25–28 minutes or until edges are bubbly and center is just lightly browned. Remove from oven and immediately run a narrow metal spatula or table knife around edges of pan to loosen. Cool completely in pan on a wire rack; cut into bars.

Makes 36 bars.

Italian Cheesecake Bars

With their smooth Italian accent, these rich bars are just the thing for special luncheons or afternoon chats over coffee. For a sophisticated supper conclusion, treat your guests to small cups of steaming espresso and bite-sized squares of these rich and creamy cookies.

1	18-ounce roll refrigerated sugar cookie dough, well chilled
1	15-ounce container ricotta cheese
1	large egg
⅓	cup granulated sugar
2	tablespoons all-purpose flour
2	teaspoons finely shredded orange peel
1	teaspoon almond extract
½	cup golden raisins (or dried cranberries), chopped
½	cup sliced almonds (or chopped hazelnuts)

- Preheat oven to 350°. Spray a 13 x 9-inch pan with nonstick cooking spray or line with foil.

- Cut cookie dough into ¼-inch-thick slices. Arrange slices in bottom of the prepared pan. With floured fingers, press dough evenly to form crust.

- Bake 10–13 minutes or until dough is golden brown (dough will appear slightly puffed). Remove from oven.

- In a medium bowl whisk the ricotta cheese, egg, sugar, flour, orange peel, and almond extract until smooth; stir in raisins. Carefully spread cheese mixture over warm crust; sprinkle with almonds.

- Bake 22–25 minutes or until edges are puffed and golden. Cool in pan on a wire rack for 1 hour; cover and chill for 2 hours. Cut into bars; store in refrigerator.

Makes 36 bars.

Carmelitas

*For a few selfish moments I came close to dubbing these scrumptious bakehouse bars
"Camilla-litas." Of all the cookies in this book, I could easily eat these every day without
ever tiring of them. I prefer them with milk chocolate chips, but I have also made them
with butterscotch, white chocolate, and cinnamon chips, all to rave reviews.*

1	18-ounce roll refrigerated sugar cookie dough
1½	cups quick-cooking or old-fashioned oats
¼	cup firmly packed dark brown sugar
1	cup chopped pecans (or walnuts)
1	cup milk (or semisweet) chocolate chips
1	12-ounce jar (about 1 cup) caramel ice cream topping

- Preheat oven to 350°. Spray a a 9-inch pan with nonstick cooking
spray or line with foil.

- Crumble cookie dough into large bowl; add oats and brown sugar. Mix
with wooden spoon or your fingers until combined. Press half of mixture into bottom of the prepared pan.

- Bake 10-13 minutes or until dough is golden brown (dough will
appear slightly puffed). Remove from oven.

- Sprinkle chocolate chips and nuts evenly over crust; drizzle with
caramel sauce. Sprinkle the reserved oat mixture evenly over the top;
press gently with fingertips to form an even layer.

- Return the pan to the oven and continue baking until the topping is
golden brown and firm to the touch, about 18–21 minutes longer.
Remove the pan to a wire rack and cool completely. Cut into bars.

Makes 16 small or 9 big bars.

Blackberry Cheesecake Bars

The popularity of cheesecake doesn't seem to end. Thank goodness. This version gives the tried and true classic a contrasting cookie base and a delicious swirl of blackberry jam. Cut them small and serve in the most casual of circumstances or cut them big and plate them with a handful of fresh berries for a sophisticated dinner finale.

1	18-ounce roll refrigerated sugar cookie dough, well chilled
2	8-ounce packages cream cheese, softened
⅔	cup granulated sugar
2	large eggs
1	teaspoon vanilla extract
¾	cup blackberry (or other fruit) preserves, room temperature

- Preheat oven to 350°. Spray a 13 x 9-inch pan with nonstick cooking spray or line with foil.

- Cut cookie dough into ¼-inch-thick slices. Arrange slices in bottom of the prepared pan. With floured fingers, press dough evenly to form crust.

- Bake 10–13 minutes or until dough is golden brown (dough will appear slightly puffed). Remove from oven.

- Meanwhile, in a medium bowl beat the cream cheese and sugar with electric beaters on high until smooth. Add eggs and vanilla; beat until just combined.

- Evenly spread cream cheese mixture over hot cookie base; dollop with teaspoons of blackberry jam. Swirl cream cheese filling and jam slightly with the tip of a knife.

- Bake in middle of oven until slightly puffed, about 22–25 minutes. Cool completely in pan and cut into bars; chill.

Baker's Note: The preserves will be easier to swirl if they are room temperature instead of chilled.

Makes 24 big bars.

Coffee Toffee Chocolate Bars

Prepare to go nuts for these rocky-topped bars. Make a batch whenever you need to celebrate—coffee breaks included.

1   18-ounce roll refrigerated sugar cookie dough, well chilled
1   14-ounce can sweetened condensed milk
2   tablespoons butter
1   tablespoon coffee liqueur
2   teaspoons instant espresso (or coffee) powder
1   cup chopped pecans (or walnuts)
1   cup chopped chocolate-covered espresso beans
1   cup coarsely chopped chocolate-covered English toffee
    candy bars

Preheat oven to 350°. Spray a 13 x 9-inch pan with nonstick cooking spray or line with foil.

Cut cookie dough into ¼-inch-thick slices. Arrange slices in bottom of the prepared pan. With floured fingers, press dough evenly to form crust.

Bake 10–13 minutes or until dough is golden brown (dough will appear slightly puffed). Remove from oven.

Meanwhile, in a medium, heavy saucepan combine the condensed milk and butter. Bring to a boil over medium heat; cook and stir 5 minutes. Remove from heat and stir in liqueur and espresso powder. Pour mixture over partially baked crust; sprinkle with nuts.

Bake in middle of oven until slightly puffed, about 12 minutes. Remove from oven and immediately sprinkle with chopped espresso beans and toffee bars; gently press mixture into uncut bars. Cool completely; chill. Let stand 5 minutes before cutting into bars.

Makes 48 bars.

Bar Cookies

Pecan Pie Bars

Everything you love about pecan pie—perhaps the most famous of all the decadent Southern desserts—is captured in these foolproof bar cookies. Cut them small to serve as bite-sized delights, or cut into big squares to serve "pie style" with vanilla ice cream or whipped cream.

1	18-ounce roll refrigerated sugar cookie dough, well chilled
4	large eggs
1	cup packed brown sugar
1	cup dark corn syrup
½	stick (¼ cup) butter, melted
1	teaspoon vanilla extract
2	cups chopped pecans

- Preheat oven to 350°. Spray a 13 x 9-inch pan with nonstick cooking spray or line with foil.

- Cut cookie dough into ¼-inch-thick slices. Arrange slices in bottom of the prepared pan. With floured fingers, press dough evenly to form crust.

- Bake 10–13 minutes or until dough is golden brown (dough will appear slightly puffed). Remove from oven.

- In a medium bowl whisk the eggs, brown sugar, corn syrup, melted butter, and vanilla until blended; stir in pecans. Pour pecan mixture over warm, partially baked crust and spread evenly.

- Bake 25–30 minutes or until filling is just set. Cool completely in pan and cut into bars.

Baker's Note: Chocolate lover? Substitute chocolate-chip cookie dough for the sugar cookie dough in this recipe. Proceed as directed.

Makes 36 bars.

Bananas Foster Bars

A sprinkle of rum extract imparts a note of extravagance to the bananas in these bars; rich, buttery caramel adds a layer of luxury.

- 1 8-ounce package cream cheese, softened
- ½ cup mashed, ripe banana (about 1 medium banana)
- 1½ tablespoons all-purpose flour
- 6 tablespoons thick caramel ice cream topping, divided
- 1 large egg yolk
- 1½ teaspoons rum (or brandy) extract
- 1 18-ounce roll refrigerated sugar cookie dough, well chilled
- ½ cup chopped pecans

- Preheat oven to 350°. Spray an 8- or 9-inch baking pan with nonstick spray or line with foil.

- In a medium bowl beat cream cheese, mashed banana, flour, 2 tablespoons caramel topping, egg yolk, and rum extract with electric beaters until smooth; set aside.

- Cut cookie dough in half. Press half of the dough in bottom of the prepared pan. Spread cream cheese mixture over dough. Crumble and sprinkle remaining half of cookie dough and pecans over cream cheese mixture; gently press into cream cheese layer.

- Bake 33–36 minutes or until golden brown and firm to the touch. Cool completely. Drizzle with remaining 4 tablespoons caramel topping. Cut into bars. Serve room temperature or chilled. Store in refrigerator.

Baker's Note: For a chocolate twist, use chocolate-chip cookie dough in place of sugar cookie dough.

Makes 16 bars.

Bar Cookies

Burst of Lime Bars

Imagine your favorite silken lemon bar; add a twist of lime and a kick of ginger and you know what this bar tastes like. It's an incomparable cookie for any occasion with an incredible flavor unlike any other.

1	18-ounce roll refrigerated sugar cookie dough, well chilled
4	large eggs
1½	cups granulated sugar
¾	cup fresh lime juice
⅓	cup all-purpose flour
1	teaspoon ground ginger
3	tablespoons sifted powdered sugar

- Preheat oven to 350°. Spray a 13 x 9-inch pan with nonstick cooking spray or line with foil.

- Cut cookie dough into ¼-inch-thick slices. Arrange slices in bottom of the prepared pan. With floured fingers, press dough evenly to form crust.

- Bake 10–13 minutes or until light golden brown (dough will appear slightly puffed). Remove from oven.

- Meanwhile, in a medium bowl whisk together eggs and granulated sugar until blended; whisk in lime juice, flour, and ginger. Pour mixture over warm, partially baked crust.

- Reduce oven temperature to 300° and bake bars in middle of oven until just set, about 30 minutes. Cool completely in pan; cut into bars. Sift powdered sugar over bars before serving.

Makes 36 bars.

Chocolate-Chip Cookie Dough Brownies

These cookie dough–filled brownies effortlessly pass the "devour in the middle of the night" test. Be careful not to overbake—the cookie dough should maintain a slight ooey-gooey quality when the brownies are done.

1	19½ -ounce package brownie mix
2	large eggs
¼	cup water
½	cup vegetable oil
1	18-ounce roll refrigerated chocolate-chip cookie dough, well chilled
1	recipe Dark Chocolate Frosting, see page 211, (optional)

• Preheat oven to 350°. Spray a 13 x 9-inch pan with nonstick cooking spray or line with foil.

• In a medium mixing bowl mix brownie mix, eggs, water, and oil with a wooden spoon until well blended. Spread batter into the prepared pan.

• Break up cookie dough into walnut-size pieces; drop evenly onto brownie batter, pressing down lightly.

• Bake 37–40 minutes or until a toothpick inserted two inches from side of pan comes out almost clean. Cool completely. If desired, spread with Dark Chocolate Frosting.

Makes 48 brownies.

White Chocolate & Lime-Layered Bars

These luscious layered bars carry a double dose of lime. For a heavenly summer dessert, cut the bars into larger squares or diamonds and serve with berries and a cloud of whipped cream.

1	18-ounce roll refrigerated sugar cookie dough, well chilled
1½	cups unsweetened shredded coconut
1	cup sliced almonds
1	14-ounce can sweetened condensed milk
2½	tablespoons lime juice
2	teaspoons grated lime zest
2	cups white chocolate chips

- Preheat oven to 350°. Spray a 13 x 9-inch pan with nonstick cooking spray or line with foil.

- Cut cookie dough into ¼-inch-thick slices. Arrange slices in bottom of the prepared pan. With floured fingers, press dough evenly to form crust.

- Bake 10–14 minutes or until light golden brown (dough will appear slightly puffed).

- Sprinkle coconut and almonds over partially baked crust. In a small bowl combine condensed milk, lime juice, and lime zest. Drizzle mixture over coconut and almonds.

- Bake for 21–24 minutes or until edges are golden brown and top is lightly browned. Remove from oven and immediately sprinkle with white chocolate chips. Cool completely. Cut into bars.

Makes 36 bars.

4 Filled Cookies

If a delicate, elegant, and slightly dainty cookie is what you're after, you've flipped to the right chapter. Although this category of cookies includes thumbprints, spirals, sandwich cookies, tassies, and tartlets, the basic formula is the same: a delicious filling encased by cookie dough. The fillings vary from jam, jelly, peanut butter, marshmallow creme, miniature chocolate candy bars, to cream cheese and may be rolled into, wrapped inside, or dollopped onto the dough.

Filled cookies traditionally take longer to prepare, but not so here. Starting with refrigerated cookie dough for these fanciful cookies is a special boon because it cuts out multiple steps. And the results? Ooh la la. Prepare for an ambush if these cookies go unguarded.

"Pick Your Filling" Thumbprints

With just two ingredients and minimal preparation steps, this is one of the handiest cook-ies to make. Children can help in the production by making the "thumbprint" in each warm cookie and filling the impressions with any number of delicious options.

1 **18-ounce roll refrigerated chocolate-chip cookie dough, well chilled**
½ **cup filling of choice (see options below)**

- Preheat oven to 350°. Spray cookie sheets with nonstick cooking spray.
- Cut cookie dough into 12 equal slices. Cut each slice in half. Roll each piece into a ball. Place balls two inches apart on cookie sheets.
- Bake 10–12 minutes or until golden at edges.
- Remove cookies from oven and immediately make a depression in each cookie with thumb or cork; fill each with spoonful of filling. Transfer to wire racks and cool completely.

Filling options:
- *Any flavor preserves, jam, jelly, marmalade, or apple butter*
- *Lemon curd*
- *Smooth-style peanut butter*
- *Chocolate-hazelnut spread*
- *Sweetened soft-spread style cream cheese, any flavor*
- *Canned cake frosting, any flavor*

Baker's Note: If using cream cheese as a filling, be sure to store cookies in refrigerator.

Makes 24 cookies.

"Pick Your Filling" Cookie Sandwiches

Satisfy your kid cravings with these yummy cookies, personalized with your favorite filling. Try filling them with any one of the thick frosting recipes in Chapter 6—such as Irish Cream or Dark Chocolate Frosting. Or use any one of the "no-prep" fillings, such as peanut butter or canned cake frosting.

1   18-ounce roll refrigerated chocolate-chip cookie dough (or sugar cookie dough), well chilled
1   recipe frosting of your choice, see Chapter 6, (or 1¼ cups "no-prep" filling of your choice, see page 202)

- Preheat oven to 350°. Spray cookie sheets with nonstick cooking spray.

- With a sharp knife cut cookie dough crosswise into 4 equal pieces; cut each piece into 8 equal slices. Arrange slices two inches apart on cookie sheets.

- Bake 8–11 minutes or until golden at edges and just set at the center. Transfer to wire racks and cool completely.

- Generously spread bottom side of one cookie with frosting or filling of choice; place second cookie, bottom side down, on top. Gently press together. Repeat with remaining cookies and marshmallow mixture.

Baker's Note: If using cream cheese as a filling, be sure to store cookies in refrigerator.

Makes 16 cookie sandwiches.

Filled Cookies

Eggnog Thumbprints

These delicately spiced cookies are bound to stir up memories of favorite holidays spent with family and friends. Be sure to store them in the refrigerator once they are filled.

½   cup soft spread-style honey nut cream cheese
¾   teaspoon rum extract
¾   teaspoon nutmeg, divided
1   teaspoon cinnamon
⅓   cup granulated sugar
1   18-ounce roll refrigerated sugar cookie dough, well chilled

• Preheat oven to 350°. Spray cookie sheets with nonstick cooking spray.

• In a small bowl mix cream cheese, rum extract, and ¼ teaspoon nutmeg; mix well and set aside.

• In a small dish combine cinnamon, remaining ½ teaspoon nutmeg and sugar.

• Cut cookie dough into 12 equal slices. Cut each slice in half. Roll each piece into a ball; roll balls in sugar mixture. Place balls two inches apart on cookie sheets.

• Bake 10–12 minutes or until golden at edges.

• Remove cookies from oven and immediately make a depression in each cookie with thumb or cork; fill each with spoonful of cream cheese mixture. Transfer to wire racks and cool completely. Store in refrigerator.

Makes 24 cookies.

Lemon Coconut Thumbprints

The combination of citrus and toasted coconut coalesce to create this scrumptious summer cookie, perfect for pairing with long, cold glasses of iced tea or lemonade.

1   18-ounce roll refrigerated sugar cookie dough, well chilled
¾   cup shredded coconut
½   cup lemon curd (or canned lemon pie filling)
½   cup white chocolate chips
1   teaspoon vegetable shortening

- Preheat oven to 350°. Spray cookie sheets with nonstick cooking spray.

- Cut cookie dough into 12 equal slices. Cut each slice in half. Roll each piece into a ball.

- Place coconut into shallow dish; roll balls in coconut, pressing gently so that coconut adheres. Place balls two inches apart on cookie sheets.

- Bake 10–12 minutes or until coconut turns light golden.

- Remove cookies from oven and immediately make a depression in each cookie with thumb or cork; fill each with spoonful of lemon curd or pie filling. Transfer to wire racks and cool completely.

- Meanwhile, melt chips with shortening in a small saucepan set over low heat, stirring until melted and smooth. Drizzle over cookies.

Makes 24 cookies.

Filled Cookies

Baklava Bites

This recipe is based on one of my favorite desserts: baklava. For anyone who shares my affection for the flavorsome combination of nuts, spices, and honey, but fears working with phyllo dough, this is your sweet solution.

¼ cup (½ stick) butter
½ cup sifted powdered sugar
3 tablespoons honey
¾ cup finely chopped almonds (or walnuts)
¼ teaspoon cinnamon
1 teaspoon finely chopped lemon zest
1 18-ounce roll refrigerated sugar cookie dough, well chilled

● In a medium, heavy saucepan over medium heat melt the butter and then stir in the powdered sugar and honey. Cook and stir until mixture boils; remove from heat. Stir in the nuts, cinnamon, and lemon zest. Cool 30 minutes. Shape mixture by teaspoons into ½-inch balls.

● Preheat oven to 350°. Spray cookie sheets with nonstick cooking spray.

● Cut cookie dough into 12 equal slices. Cut each slice in half. Roll each piece into a ball. Place balls two inches apart on cookie sheets.

● Bake 6 minutes; remove from oven and press 1 nut ball into center of each cookie. Bake 6–7 minutes more until golden at edges.

● Transfer to wire racks and cool completely.

Makes 24 cookies.

Apricot Milk Chocolate Thumbprints

Typically unassuming little cookies, thumbprints go glamorous in this delectable combination of apricot and milk chocolate, accented with a smidgeon of nutmeg. They make a great finish for a sit-down dinner party. The problem here is keeping enough around until the guests arrive. This justifies making a double batch.

1	18-ounce roll refrigerated sugar cookie dough, well chilled
⅓	cup sugar
1	teaspoon nutmeg
½	cup apricot preserves
1	recipe Milk Chocolate Drizzle, see page 201

- Preheat oven to 350°. Spray cookie sheets with nonstick cooking spray.

- Cut cookie dough into 12 equal slices. Cut each slice in half. Roll each piece into a ball.

- In a shallow dish combine the sugar and nutmeg; roll balls in sugar mixture. Place balls two inches apart on the prepared cookie sheets.

- Bake 10–12 minutes or until light golden at edges.

- Remove cookies from oven and immediately make a depression in each cookie with thumb or cork; fill each with spoonful of apricot preserves. Transfer to wire racks and cool completely.

- Prepare Milk Chocolate Drizzle; drizzle over cookies. Place in refrigerator until chocolate is set.

Makes 24 cookies.

Filled Cookies

Cherry Chocolate Thumbprints

Cherries are great with chocolate and thumbprints are just plain great. Hence, this is nothing short of a great cookie, by any measure.

⅓   cup sugar
1½ teaspoons cinnamon
1   18-ounce roll refrigerated sugar cookie dough, well chilled
⅓   cup miniature semisweet chocolate chips
½   cup cherry preserves

- Preheat oven to 350°. Spray cookie sheets with nonstick cooking spray.

- In a small dish combine sugar and cinnamon.

- Cut cookie dough into 12 equal slices. Cut each slice in half. Roll each piece into a ball; roll balls in sugar mixture. Place balls two inches apart on cookie sheets.

- Bake 10–12 minutes or until golden at edges.

- Remove cookies from oven and immediately make a depression in each cookie with thumb or cork; fill each with ½ teaspoon of miniature chocolate chips; return to oven for 30 seconds.

- Remove cookies from oven and place a teaspoon of preserves on top of the chocolate filling. Transfer to wire racks and cool completely.

Makes 24 cookies.

Blackberry Sage Thumbprints

Blackberries and sage? Absolutely. This cookie was inspired by one of my favorite teas of the same name. The combination of the earthy flavor of sage and the bright flavor of blackberry is a winning match.

- ⅓   cup sugar
- 2   teaspoons rubbed dry sage
- 1   18-ounce roll refrigerated sugar cookie dough, well chilled
- ½   cup blackberry preserves or jam

- Preheat oven to 350°. Spray cookie sheets with nonstick cooking spray.

- In a small dish combine the sugar and sage; set aside.

- Cut cookie dough into 12 equal slices. Cut each slice in half. Roll each piece into a ball; roll balls in sugar mixture. Place balls two inches apart on cookie sheets.

- Bake 10–12 minutes or until golden at edges.

- Remove cookies from oven and immediately make a depression in each cookie with thumb or cork; fill each with a teaspoon of jam.

- Transfer to wire racks and cool completely.

Makes 24 cookies.

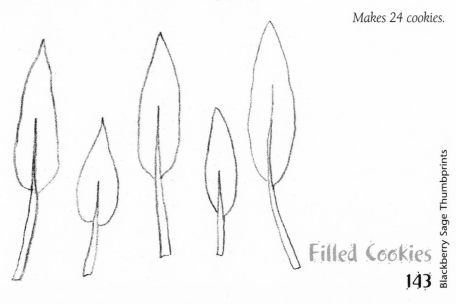

Filled Cookies

Nutty Jam Gems

A generous coating of nuts adds just the right amount of crunch to transform these bite-sized morsels into jam-filled treasures.

- 1   18-ounce roll refrigerated sugar cookie dough, well chilled
- 1   cup finely chopped almonds, pecans, walnuts, or peanuts
- ½   cup jam or preserves, any flavor

- Preheat oven to 350°. Spray cookie sheets with nonstick cooking spray.
- Cut cookie dough into 12 equal slices. Cut each slice in half. Roll each piece into a ball.
- Place chopped nuts into a shallow dish; roll balls in the nuts, pressing gently so that the nuts adhere. Place balls two inches apart on prepared cookie sheets.
- Bake 10–12 minutes or until golden at edges.
- Remove cookies from oven and immediately make a depression in each cookie with thumb or cork; fill each with a spoonful of preserves. Transfer to wire racks and cool completely.

Makes 24 cookies.

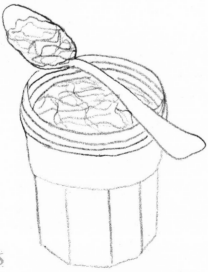

Raspberry Tart Cookies

This recipe reminds me of a far more complicated cookie my mother made every Christmas of my childhood. Besides their winning flavor, I remember her making a double batch since we ate about half of the cookies straight from the oven. At once both no-nonsense and elegant, they can be made with any jam or preserve of your choosing. To dress them up further, dust them with sifted powdered sugar just before serving.

1 18-ounce roll refrigerated sugar cookie dough, well chilled
½ cup seedless raspberry jam or preserves

- Preheat oven to 350°. Spray cookie sheets with nonstick cooking spray.

- Cut dough in half; refrigerate remaining dough. With sharp knife, cut dough half into 24 thin slices. Place slices two inches apart on cookie sheets.

- Place 1 teaspoon jam in center of each cookie slice. Set aside momentarily.

- Cut remaining dough into 24 thin slices. Place cookie slices on jam-topped cookie slices; press edges with tines of fork to decorate and seal.

- Bake 10–12 minutes or until edges are light golden brown. Cool 1 minute on cookie sheets. Transfer to wire racks and cool completely.

Baker's Note: For a decorative flair, cut 1-inch star shape out of center of each top cookie slice. Proceed as above. To bake the tiny star cut-outs, place on a cookie sheet and bake 4–6 minutes.

Makes 24 cookies.

Chocolate Candy Treasure Cookies

What happens when you cover a candy bar nugget in sugar cookie dough and bake it until silken in the center? Magic. Even though it is a test of will to wait for these treasures, be sure to let them cool completely before serving.

1   18-ounce roll refrigerated sugar cookie dough, well chilled
12   miniature peanut butter cup (or any chocolate-covered nugget-size candies), unwrapped
½   cup semisweet chocolate chips
1   teaspoon vegetable shortening

- Preheat oven to 350°. Spray cookie sheets with nonstick cooking spray.

- Cut cookie dough into 12 equal pieces. Wrap 1 piece of dough around each candy, completely covering candy; roll in hands to form ball.

- Place 6 dough balls on cookie sheet. Refrigerate remaining 6 dough balls until ready to bake.

- Bake 12–15 minutes or until golden brown. Cool 2 minutes on cookie sheets. Transfer to wire racks and cool completely. Repeat with remaining 6 dough balls.

- In small saucepan over low heat, combine chocolate chips and shortening; cook over low heat until melted and smooth, stirring constantly. Drizzle over cooled cookies in crisscross pattern. Let stand until glaze is set before storing.

Makes 12 big cookies.

Russian Sour Cream Tarts

Rich and elegant, this is a cookie for company. Be sure the almonds are absolutely fresh for the best flavor—a good sniff test for staleness will work. To heighten their flavor, toast the nuts in a 350° oven for 8–10 minutes until fragrant. Cool the nuts completely before chopping and adding to the recipe.

1	18-ounce roll refrigerated sugar cookie dough, well chilled
1¼	cups blanched almonds, finely chopped
2	tablespoons powdered sugar
3	tablespoons sour cream
2	tablespoons apricot preserves
2	large eggs, separated
¼	cup granulated sugar

• Preheat oven to 350°. Spray cookie sheets with nonstick cookie spray.

• With a sharp knife cut cookie dough crosswise into 4 equal pieces; cut each piece into 7 equal slices. Arrange slices two inches apart on cookie sheets.

• In a small bowl combine the almonds, powdered sugar, sour cream, preserves, and egg yolks; mix well. Spoon and spread 1 teaspoon filling onto each cookie slice.

• In a small bowl beat egg whites until soft peaks form. Gradually add sugar, beating until stiff peaks form. Top each cookie with 1 teaspoon meringue; swirl top.

• Bake 10–12 minutes or until meringue is lightly golden brown. Transfer to wire racks and cool completely.

Makes 28 cookies.

Filled Cookies

147

Lemony Hidden Kiss Cookies

When I'm feeling self-indulgent on trips home to California, I stop in at a small bakery just blocks from my parents' home. There I pick up a double mocha (with extra whipped cream) and one of their specialties, a lemon cookie drizzled with milk chocolate. This is my own sweet version. The milk chocolate is both snuggled inside the dough and drizzled on top.

1 **18-ounce roll refrigerated sugar cookie dough, well chilled**
1 **teaspoon lemon extract**
20 **milk chocolate candy kisses, unwrapped**
½ **cup milk (or semisweet) chocolate chips**
1 **tablespoon vegetable shortening**

- Preheat oven to 375°. Spray cookie sheets with nonstick cooking spray.

- Crumble cookie dough into large bowl. Sprinkle with lemon extract; mix well with fingers or wooden spoon.

- Shape about 1 tablespoon dough around each candy kiss, covering completely. Roll in hands to form a ball; place on cookie sheets.

- Bake 8–11 minutes or until cookies are set and bottoms are light golden brown. Cool 1 minute on sheets. Transfer to wire racks and cool completely.

- In a small saucepan combine chocolate chips and shortening; cook and stir over low heat until melted and smooth. Drizzle over cooled cookies. Let stand until set. Store in tightly covered container.

Baker's Note: You can use any other flavor of extract—orange, maple, mint, rum, brandy—in place of the lemon, or leave it out altogether.

Makes 20 cookies.

Chocolate-Filled Aztec Cookies

Offer a plate of these cookies along with an assortment of fresh fruit as a fitting finale to a Mexican-style meal. Leftovers are great additions to weekday lunchbags, too.

- 1 18-ounce roll refrigerated sugar cookie dough, well chilled
- ¼ cup yellow cornmeal
- ¾ teaspoon ground cinnamon
- ⅛ teaspoon ground cayenne pepper
- 1 teaspoon finely chopped orange zest
- 20 dark chocolate candy miniatures, unwrapped

- Preheat oven to 375°. Spray cookie sheets with nonstick cooking spray.

- Crumble cookie dough into large bowl. Let stand 10–15 minutes to soften. Add cornmeal, cinnamon, cayenne, and orange zest; mix well with fingers or wooden spoon.

- Shape rounded tablespoon of dough around each candy, covering completely. Place two inches apart on cookie sheets.

- Bake 8–11 minutes or until edges are light golden brown. Cool 1 minute on sheets. Transfer to wire racks and cool completely.

Makes 20 cookies.

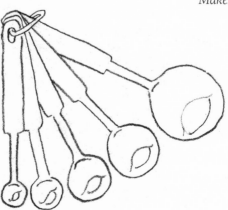

Filled Cookies

Fluffer-Nutter Chocolate-Chip Cookie Sandwiches

Peanut butter and marshmallow? Oh yes. Fluffer-nutter aficionados know that something so right can never be wrong. Here the traditional peanut butter and marshmallow fluff sandwich gets a new-fangled twist with chocolate-chip cookies in place of white bread.

1	**18-ounce roll refrigerated chocolate-chip cookie dough, well chilled**
½	**cup creamy-style peanut butter**
1	**cup marshmallow creme**

- Preheat oven to 350°. Line two 8-inch pans with foil; spray with non-stick cooking spray.

- Cut cookie dough into ¼-inch-thick slices. Divide slices between the two pans. With floured fingers, press dough evenly to form crust.

- Bake 13–17 minutes or until golden brown and set at the center. Remove from oven and cool completely.

- Use foil to lift cookies from pans; remove foil.

- Place cookies, bottom side up, on work surface. Spread one cookie with peanut butter; spread second cookie with marshmallow creme.

- Place cookie, marshmallow creme side down, on top of peanut butter-spread cookie. Cut into 16 pieces. Wrap each in plastic wrap or foil. Store in refrigerator to keep filling firm.

Makes 16 cookie sandwiches.

Charlotte's Date-Filled Cookie Tarts

To this day my mother reminisces about the brown sugar tarts she ate as a child on afternoon tea trips to downtown Winnipeg. This streamlined rendition is just for her. You don't have to love dates—just the unmistakable flavor combination of brown sugar and butter—to love these cookie tarts.

- ½ **cup chopped dates**
- ¼ **cup packed brown sugar**
- 2 **tablespoons butter**
- 2 **tablespoons water**
- 1 **18-ounce roll refrigerated sugar cookie dough, well chilled**

- In a medium saucepan combine the dates, brown sugar, butter, and water. Bring to a boil over medium-high heat; reduce heat to low and simmer 10 minutes, stirring frequently. Transfer to a small bowl and cool completely.

- Preheat oven to 350°. Spray cookie sheets with nonstick cooking spray.

- Cut dough in half; refrigerate remaining dough. With sharp knife, cut dough half into 24 thin slices. Place slices two inches apart on cookie sheets.

- Place 1 generous teaspoon cooled date mixture in center of each cookie slice. Set aside.

- Cut remaining dough into 24 thin slices. Place cookie slices on jam-topped cookie slices; press edges with tines of fork to decorate and seal.

- Bake 10–12 minutes or until edges are light golden brown. Cool 1 minute on cookie sheets. Transfer to wire racks and cool completely.

Makes 24 cookies.

Filled Cookies

S'more Sandwiches

The original campfire treat undergoes a tasty transformation in this easy chocolate-chip sandwich cookie.

1   18-ounce roll refrigerated chocolate-chip cookie dough, well chilled
1   cup sifted powdered sugar
1   7-ounce jar (about 1½ cups) marshmallow creme

- Preheat oven to 350°. Spray cookie sheets with nonstick cooking spray.

- With a sharp knife cut cookie dough crosswise into 4 equal pieces; cut each piece into 8 equal slices. Arrange slices two inches apart on cookie sheets.

- Bake 8–11 minutes or until golden at edges and just set at the center. Transfer to wire racks and cool completely.

- Meanwhile, in a medium bowl combine the powdered sugar and marshmallow creme; mix with wooden spoon until well blended.

- Place 1 heaping tablespoon marshmallow mixture on bottom side of one cookie; place second cookie, bottom side down, on top. Gently press together. Repeat with remaining cookies and marshmallow mixture.

Makes 16 cookie sandwiches.

Stacked, Packed Peanut Butter-Fudge Chocolate Chippers

This just may be the quintessential indulgence for chocolate and peanut butter lovers.

2   18-ounce rolls refrigerated chocolate-chip cookie dough, well chilled
1   cup canned chocolate cake frosting
¾   cup creamy peanut butter

- Preheat oven to 350°. Spray cookie sheets with nonstick cooking spray.

- With a sharp knife cut each cookie dough roll crosswise into 4 equal pieces; cut each piece into 8 equal slices. Arrange slices two inches apart on cookie sheets.

- Bake 8–11 minutes or until golden at edges and just set at the center. Transfer to wire racks and cool completely.

- In small bowl combine frosting and peanut butter; blend well. Spread about 1 heaping tablespoon peanut butter–fudge mixture on bottom side of each cookie; top each with a second cookie, bottom side down. Press gently. Store in refrigerator.

Makes 32 sandwich cookies.

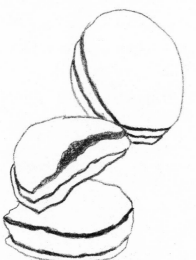

Filled Cookies

Chocolate-Raisin Cookie Tartlets

Serve these rich chocolate tartlets warm or cold. They are perfect with coffee at the end of dinner, or out in the sunshine on a springtime picnic. Chopped dried cranberries or apricots can be substituted for the raisins.

½   **cup chopped raisins**
½   **cup water**
¼   **cup firmly packed brown sugar**
½   **teaspoon grated orange peel**
¼   **cup semisweet chocolate chips**
1   **18-ounce roll refrigerated sugar cookie dough, well chilled**

- In small saucepan combine the raisins, water, brown sugar, and orange peel. Bring to a boil. Cook over low heat 11–13 minutes or until liquid is almost completely absorbed, stirring frequently. Remove from heat and immediately stir in chocolate chips. Cool completely.

- Preheat oven to 350°. Spray cookie sheets with nonstick cooking spray.

- Cut dough in half crosswise; refrigerate remaining dough. With sharp knife, cut dough half into 20 thin slices. Place slices two inches apart on cookie sheets. Place 1 generous teaspoon chocolate-raisin mixture in center of each cookie slice. Set aside.

- Cut remaining dough into 20 thin slices. Place cookie slices on filling-topped cookie slices; press edges with tines of fork to decorate and seal.

- Bake 10–12 minutes or until edges are light golden brown. Cool 1 minute on cookie sheets. Transfer to wire racks and cool completely.

Baker's Note: Other chopped dried fruit, such as dried cranberries or dried apricots, may be substituted for the chopped raisins.

Makes 20 cookies.

Fast and Fudgy Mini Tarts

These scrumptious bites of fudge are as impressive as they are easy to prepare. For a holiday-inspired peppermint variation, substitute ½ teaspoon mint extract for the vanilla extract. Garnish each chocolate mint tart with crushed red and white peppermint candies.

1   **18-ounce roll refrigerated sugar cookie dough, well chilled**
1   **cup semisweet chocolate chips**
½   **cup canned sweetened condensed milk**
½   **teaspoon vanilla extract**

- Preheat oven to 350°. Spray 24 mini muffin pan cups (1¾-inch size) with nonstick cooking spray.

- Slice cookie dough in half; refrigerate half. Cut remaining half into 6 equal pieces; cut each piece into 4 equal pieces (a total of 24 pieces). Press each dough piece into bottoms and up the sides of prepared muffin cups.

- Bake dough cups 8–10 minutes or until golden (dough will not be completely set). Remove from oven and press an indentation into center of each cup with the back of a ½-teaspoon measuring spoon.

- Bake 2 minutes longer until golden. Place pans on wire racks and cool 15–20 minutes. Carefully remove tart cups from the pans.

- Remove second half of dough from refrigerator and repeat, making a total of 48 cups. Cool all cups completely while making filling.

- In a small saucepan over medium-high heat, combine the chocolate chips and condensed milk. Cook and stir until chocolate melts and mixture is smooth; stir in vanilla.

- Fill each tart cup with a teaspoon of filling. Let stand until filling sets.

> Baker's Note: If you only want or need half a batch of tarts, follow all of the directions above but halve the ingredients. Make one batch of tart cups (24 total) and proceed as directed above. Wrap and freeze the second half of dough for a future batch of biscotti or cookies.

Makes 48 mini-tarts.

Filled Cookies

Ginger & Lime Cheesecake Tartlets

I enjoyed the most delicious cheesecake ever at one of the most unlikely spots: a food court at a mall in Indianapolis. Turns out the proprietor's mother supplied the sandwich stand's scrumptious desserts. These mini ginger-lime gems are my best approximation of the remarkable slice of heaven I enjoyed that day.

1	18-ounce roll refrigerated sugar cookie dough, well chilled
1	8-ounce package cream cheese, softened
½	cup sweetened condensed milk
1	large egg
2	teaspoons fresh lime juice
1	teaspoon grated lime zest
1	teaspoon ground ginger

- Preheat oven to 350°. Line 12 muffin cups with paper liners.

- Slice cookie dough into 12 equal pieces. Place one piece in each muffin cup. Bake 10–12 minutes or until cookie has spread to edge of cup (dough will appear slightly puffed). Remove from the oven and press an indentation into the center of each cup with the back of a spoon.

- Meanwhile, in medium bowl combine the cream cheese, condensed milk, egg, lime juice, lime zest, and ginger; beat with an electric mixer on high until smooth. Spoon cream cheese mixture over each cookie in cup.

- Bake an additional 13–17 minutes or until cream cheese filling is just set. Cool completely in pan on wire rack. Refrigerate for 1 hour until chilled.

Makes 12 cheesecake tartlets.

Chocolate-Chip Cherry Cheesecake Tartlets

Beyond being a delicious recipe, this is also a template for any miniature cheesecake.
Vary the type of fruit topping, for example, or leave it off altogether and flavor the filling
with anything from coffee powder, citrus zest, or liqueur.

1	18-ounce roll refrigerated chocolate-chip cookie dough
1	8-ounce package cream cheese, softened
½	cup sweetened condensed milk
1	large egg
1	teaspoon vanilla extract
1	21-ounce can cherry pie filling

- Preheat oven to 325°. Line 12 muffin cups with paper liners.

- Slice cookie dough into 12 equal pieces. Place one piece in each muffin cup. Bake 10–12 minutes or until cookie has spread to edge of cup (dough will appear slightly puffed). Remove from the oven and press an indentation into the center of each cup with the back of a spoon.

- Meanwhile, in a medium bowl combine the cream cheese, condensed milk, egg, and vanilla; beat with an electric mixer on high until smooth. Spoon cream cheese mixture over each cookie in cup.

- Bake an additional 13–17 minutes or until cream cheese filling is just set. Cool completely in pan on wire rack. Top with pie filling. Refrigerate for 1 hour until chilled.

Makes 12 cheesecake tartlets.

Filled Cookies

Chocolate-Chip Cherry Cheesecake Tartlets

Maple Cinnamon Spirals

It's worth splurging on real maple syrup for this recipe—nothing else tastes quite like it. Once you experience the winning combination of maple and cinnamon in these pretty cookies, you will want to add them to your list of favorites.

1   **18-ounce roll refrigerated sugar cookie dough, well chilled**
¼   **cup granulated sugar**
1   **tablespoon ground cinnamon**
¼   **cup pure maple syrup**

- Using a lightly floured rolling pin on a lightly floured surface, roll dough into a 16 x 8-inch rectangle. In a small dish combine the sugar and cinnamon; sprinkle evenly over rolled dough.

- Starting with 16-inch side, roll up dough jelly-roll fashion; cut in half to form two 8-inch rolls. Tightly wrap each roll in plastic wrap or foil; freeze two hours until firm.

- Preheat oven to 350°. Spray cookie sheets with nonstick cooking spray.

- Using a sharp knife, cut each dough log in half crosswise; cut each piece into 8 even slices. Place slices two inches apart on prepared sheets; brush with maple syrup.

- Bake 10–13 minutes or until light golden brown and just set at centers. Immediately transfer cookies to wire cooling racks and cool completely.

Makes 32 cookies.

Cranberry-Orange Pinwheels

Here's a cookie I love to add to holiday cookie gift plates. It's a grab-bag of many of my favorite fall flavors: cranberry, orange, and allspice.

1	tablespoon cornstarch
¾	cup whole-berry cranberry sauce
¼	cup orange marmalade
¼	teaspoon allspice
1	18-ounce roll refrigerated sugar cookie dough, well chilled

- In a small saucepan combine the cornstarch, cranberry sauce, and marmalade. Bring to a boil over medium heat, stirring constantly. Transfer to a small bowl and stir in allspice. Cool completely.

- Using a lightly floured rolling pin on a lightly floured surface, roll dough into a 16 x 8-inch rectangle. Spoon and spread cooled filling evenly over dough to within ½ inch of edges.

- Starting with 16-inch side, roll up dough jelly-roll fashion; cut in half to form two 8-inch rolls. Wrap each in plastic wrap or foil; freeze for 2 hours until firm.

- Preheat oven to 350°. Spray cookie sheets with nonstick cooking spray.

- Using a sharp knife, cut each dough log in half crosswise; cut each piece into 8 even slices. Place slices two inches apart on prepared sheets.

- Bake 10–13 minutes or until light golden brown. Immediately transfer cookies to wire cooling racks and cool completely.

Makes 32 cookies.

Filled Cookies

Fruit & Nut Strudel Cookies

Utterly eye-pleasing, these well-dressed cookie twirls are a breeze to assemble. They are as fitting on a holiday dessert buffet as a summer picnic table. Be sure that the dough is very well chilled to make the rolling easy.

1	18-ounce roll refrigerated sugar cookie dough
1	cup apricot preserves
1	cup flaked sweetened coconut
1	cup chopped walnuts
½	cup raisins

- Using a lightly floured rolling pin on a lightly floured surface, roll dough into a 16 x 8-inch rectangle.

- Spread dough with preserves; sprinkle with coconut, walnuts, and raisins to within ½ inch of edges.

- Starting with 16-inch side, roll up dough jelly-roll fashion; cut in half to form two 8-inch rolls. Wrap each in plastic wrap or foil; freeze for 2 hours until firm.

- Preheat oven to 350°. Spray cookie sheets with nonstick cooking spray.

- Using a sharp knife, cut each dough log in half crosswise; cut each piece into 8 even slices. Place slices two inches apart on prepared sheets.

- Bake for 10–13 minutes or until light golden brown. Immediately transfer cookies to wire cooling racks and cool completely.

Makes 32 cookies.

Lemon Tassies

These dainty treats are fabulous for a wedding or baby shower. If summer berries are in season, top with a raspberry or blackberry and a fresh mint sprig.

1   **18-ounce package refrigerated sugar cookie dough, well chilled**
1   **cup jarred lemon curd (or canned lemon pie filling)**

• Preheat oven to 350°. Paper-line 32 miniature muffin cups.

• Cut cookie dough in quarters lengthwise. Cut each quarter into 8 pieces. Place 1 piece into each prepared muffin cup and press down center to form a small well.

• Bake 7–11 minutes or until edges are deep golden (dough will appear slightly puffed). Remove to wire racks and cool completely.

• Remove tart shells in their paper cups from tin. Fill each tart shell with spoonful of lemon curd. Chill at least 30 minutes or until ready to serve.

Baker's Note: For a pretty presentation, consider drizzling with White Chocolate Drizzle on page 201.

Makes 32 tassies.

Filled Cookies

5
Special Cookie
Dough Treats

The recipes in this chapter celebrate America's love of sweets with a variety of delights, both traditional and newly found. In this selection of easy-to-make sensations you're sure to find the perfect finale to any meal, no matter what courses have come before.

Included here are fresh fruit desserts such as Blueberry Cookie Pie, Gingered Nectarine and Mascarpone Tart, or Tropical Fruit Pizza. For something richer, consider Cookie Tiramisu, Cherry Chocolate-Chip Crumble, Kahlua Cream Tart, or Chocolate-Chip Banana Cream Torte. And if it's cool relief you're after on a sultry summer day, you cannot go wrong with Mocha Java Ice Cream-wiches or Strawberry Ice Cream Sundae Birthday Tart. This chapter's recipes merge all-time favorites and contemporary food trends with the ease and reassurance that comes from starting with refrigerated cookie dough.

Anytime Fruit Crumble

This dessert satisfies my cravings for down-home comfort at a moment's notice. Dished up warm with a melting scoop of vanilla ice cream, it's "health food" for the soul.

1	21-ounce can cherry, peach, blueberry or apple pie filling
2	18-ounce rolls refrigerated sugar cookie dough
1	cup quick or old-fashioned oats
1	teaspoon ground cinnamon
	Vanilla ice cream or Sweetened Whipped Cream, see page 218, (optional)

Preheat oven to 350°. Spray a 13 x 9-inch baking pan with nonstick cooking spray. Spoon pie filling into pan.

Crumble cookie dough into medium bowl; let stand 10–15 minutes to soften. Add oats and cinnamon; mix well with your fingers, the paddle attachment of an electric stand mixer, or a wooden spoon. Sprinkle mixture evenly over filling to cover.

Bake 24–28 minutes or until topping is a deep golden brown. Serve warm or at room temperature with vanilla ice cream or Sweetened Whipped Cream, if desired.

Makes 10 to 12 servings.

Baker's Note: To make a half batch of the cobbler, halve all of the ingredients and bake in an 8-inch square baking pan. Proceed as directed above, baking for 20–22 minutes.

Cherry Chocolate-Chip Crumble

Looking for some warm chocolate comfort to ward off the chilly weather and bring on the smiles? You've found it. When it's warm, vanilla ice cream seems the perfect go-with, but some softly whipped and sweetened cream would also be delicious.

2   21-ounce cans cherry pie filling
1   18-ounce roll refrigerated chocolate-chip cookie dough
1   cup quick or old-fashioned oats
½   teaspoon ground cinnamon
     Vanilla ice cream or Sweetened Whipped Cream, see
     page 218, (optional)

Preheat oven to 350°. Spray a 13 x 9-inch baking pan with nonstick cooking spray. Spoon pie filling into pan.

Crumble cookie dough into a medium bowl; let stand 10–15 minutes to soften. Add oats and cinnamon; mix well with your fingers, the paddle attachment of an electric stand mixer, or a wooden spoon. Sprinkle mixture evenly over filling to cover.

Bake 24–28 minutes or until top is a deep golden brown. Serve warm or at room temperature with vanilla ice cream or Sweetened Whipped Cream, if desired.

Baker's Note: To make a half batch of the cobbler, halve all of the ingredients and bake in an 8-inch square baking pan. Proceed as directed above, baking for 20–22 minutes.

Makes 10 to 12 servings.

Raspberry Linzer Tart

The treasured and traditional Viennese Linzer torte with raspberry preserves and rich almond dough is converted here into an equally wonderful, but much easier, cookie creation.

1	18-ounce roll refrigerated sugar cookie dough
½	cup finely chopped almonds
2	tablespoons all-purpose flour
¾	teaspoon cinnamon
½	teaspoon almond extract
⅔	cup seedless raspberry preserves

Preheat oven to 350°. Spray a 9-inch-square springform pan with non-stick cooking spray.

Crumble cookie dough into large bowl; let stand 10–15 minutes to soften. Sprinkle dough with almonds, flour, cinnamon, and almond extract; mix well with your fingers, the paddle attachment of an electric stand mixer, or a wooden spoon.

Reserve 1 cup of the cookie dough mixture. Press remaining cookie dough into bottom of prepared springform pan. Spoon and spread preserves over dough. Crumble reserved dough over preserves.

Bake 25–28 minutes or until topping is golden brown. Cool in pan on wire rack for 10 minutes. Remove springform ring. Cut into wedges and serve warm or cool completely.

Makes 8 to 10 servings.

Red, White, & Blue Cookie Tart

This patriotic tart is as delicious as it is beautiful. Despite its holiday-inspired title, you can serve this dessert whenever the spirit moves you.

- 1   18-ounce roll refrigerated sugar cookie dough, well chilled
- 1   8-ounce package cream cheese, softened
- ¼   cup sifted powdered sugar
- 2   teaspoons grated lemon zest
- 2   teaspoons fresh lemon juice
- 2   cups fresh raspberries
- 1½ cups fresh blueberries
- ¼   cup apple (or red currant) jelly

- Preheat oven to 350°. Spray a 12-inch pizza pan with nonstick cooking spray.

- Cut cookie dough into ¼-inch slices; arrange, overlapping slices, in the prepared pan, spacing evenly. With floured fingers, press edges of slices together to form crust.

- Bake 15–19 minutes or until deep golden brown. Transfer to wire rack and cool completely.

- In a medium bowl combine the cream cheese, powdered sugar, lemon zest, and lemon juice; beat with electric beaters on high until well blended. Spread over cooled crust.

- Arrange raspberries in large star shape in center. Arrange blueberries around raspberries.

- In a small saucepan set over low heat melt the jelly for 1–2 minutes, stirring frequently. Drizzle or brush over berries. Refrigerate 30 minutes or until set. Store in refrigerator.

Makes 10 to 12 servings.

Special Cookie Dough Treats

Dad's Peanut Butter Chocolate-Chip Cookie Tart

No one loves peanut butter more than my dad. Although he savors peanut butter in its most minimal state (straight off the spoon), he also adores it in combination with chocolate.

1   18-ounce roll refrigerated chocolate-chip cookie dough, well chilled
1   8-ounce package cream cheese, softened
¾   cup creamy peanut butter
1   cup sifted powdered sugar
3   tablespoons milk
¾   cup chocolate fudge ice cream topping, divided
⅓   cup chopped peanuts

• Preheat oven to 350°. Spray a 12-inch pizza pan with nonstick cooking spray.

• Cut cookie dough into ¼-inch slices; arrange, overlapping slices, in the prepared pan, spacing evenly. With floured fingers, press edges of slices together to form crust.

• Bake 15–19 minutes or until deep golden brown. Cool completely.

• In a medium bowl combine the cream cheese, peanut butter, powdered sugar, and milk; beat with electric beaters on high until well blended.

• Spread ½ cup of the fudge topping over cooled baked crust. Spread peanut butter mixture over top.

• In a small saucepan set over low heat warm the remaining ¼ cup fudge topping for 1–2 minutes; drizzle over tart. Sprinkle with peanuts. Refrigerate at least 30 minutes or until ready to serve. Cut into wedges.

Baker's Note: For an added, over-the-top touch, garnish with 1 cup coarsely chopped chocolate-covered peanut butter cups in addition to the chopped peanuts.

Special Cookie Dough Treats

Makes 10 to 12 servings.

Kahlua Cream Tart

Here's a showstopper that marries the oomph of espresso with the silkiness of white choco-late. The trick to this treat is to give it a good chill before serving and to wipe the knife between each cut for picture-perfect slices.

1   18-ounce roll refrigerated sugar cookie dough, well chilled
1   8-ounce package cream cheese, softened
3   tablespoons sugar
3   tablespoons Kahlua (or other coffee liqueur)
2   teaspoons instant espresso (or coffee) powder
1   large egg
1   cup white chocolate chips, divided
½   cup chopped pecans (optional)

- Preheat oven to 350°. Spray a 9- or 10-inch springform pan with non-stick cooking spray. Crumble dough into bottom of pan; with floured fingers, press dough to evenly cover bottom and 1½ inches up sides of pan.

- Bake 10–13 minutes or until partially set and light golden brown (crust will appear puffed). Using the back of a metal spoon, gently press dough down against bottom and sides of pan. Cool 15 minutes.

- Meanwhile, in a medium bowl combine the cream cheese, sugar, Kahlua, espresso powder, and egg; beat with an electric mixer on high, stopping to scrape down the sides of the bowl as needed. Stir in ½ cup of the white chocolate chips.

- Spoon and carefully spread mixture over crust. Sprinkle with remaining ½ cup white chocolate chips and pecans, if desired.

- Return to oven; bake 22–25 minutes or until filling is just barely set. Cool 10 minutes. Run knife around sides of pan to loosen; carefully remove sides of pan. Cool completely; chill in refrigerator. Store in refrigerator.

Makes 12 servings.

Special Cookie Dough Treats

Kahlua Cream Tart

Apple Cookie Crumble

This humble crumble, with its tart apple filling and cinnamon-spiced cookie topping, is what comfort food is all about.

7 cups peeled, coarsely chopped tart apples
⅔ cup firmly packed brown sugar
2 tablespoons all-purpose flour
1½ teaspoons cinnamon, divided
½ teaspoon nutmeg
2 tablespoons lemon juice
1 18-ounce roll refrigerated sugar cookie dough, well chilled
2 tablespoons sugar

Preheat oven to 350°. In a large bowl combine the apples, brown sugar, flour, 1 teaspoon of the cinnamon, nutmeg, and lemon juice; toss to coat apples. Spoon into a 13 x 9-inch baking dish. Cover with foil.

Bake apple mixture 25 minutes; remove from oven and remove foil.

Crumble cookie dough evenly over apples. In a small bowl combine sugar and remaining ½ teaspoon cinnamon; mix well. Sprinkle evenly over cookie dough.

Bake 22–25 minutes or until topping is golden brown.

Makes 10 to 12 servings.

Viennese Almond-Filled Cookie Tart

A crisp-chewy filling in a double cookie crust, this ultra-almond confection is not too sweet but very rich. Serve it sliced thin with small cups of espresso or strong coffee for an authentic Viennese coffeehouse experience. Or dish it up American-style, warm, with a scoop of vanilla ice cream.

1	18-ounce roll refrigerated sugar cookie dough, well chilled
1	cup finely chopped almonds
½	cup sugar
1	teaspoon grated lemon zest
1	large egg, slightly beaten
12	whole blanched almonds

- Preheat oven to 325°. Place cookie sheet in oven to preheat. Spray a 9-inch springform pan with nonstick cooking spray.

- Divide cookie dough in half. Crumble half of the dough into prepared springform pan. With floured fingers, press down dough to cover bottom of pan.

- In a small bowl combine the chopped almonds, sugar, lemon zest, and egg; blend well. Spread over crust to within ½ inch of sides of pan.

- Press remaining dough into ball shape. Between 2 sheets of waxed paper, press or roll dough to 9-inch round. Remove top sheet of waxed paper; place dough over filling. Remove waxed paper; press dough in place. Arrange almonds around the edge of the torte.

- Place springform pan on a cookie sheet. Bake 27–30 minutes or until top is deep golden brown. Cool 15 minutes; remove sides of pan and cool completely.

Makes 10 to 12 servings.

Special Cookie Dough Treats

Peach Melba Crisp

Auguste Escoffier, one of the greatest chefs the world has ever known, created a dessert of poached peach halves, vanilla ice cream, and raspberry sauce in honor of Australian opera singer Dame Nellie Melba. This homey crisp captures the same delectable combination of peaches and raspberry in all-American cobbler form.

⅔   cup sugar
½   teaspoon ground cinnamon
3   tablespoons cornstarch
1   16-ounce package frozen unsweetened sliced peaches, thawed
1   16-ounce package frozen unsweetened raspberries, thawed and drained
1   18-ounce roll refrigerated sugar cookie dough, well chilled
    Sweetened Whipped cream, see page 218, or vanilla ice cream (optional)

- Preheat oven to 375°. Spray a 13 x 9-inch pan with nonstick cooking spray.

- In large bowl blend together the sugar, cinnamon, and cornstarch with a wire whisk. Add the peaches and raspberries; mix well. Pour into the prepared pan.

- Crumble cookie dough evenly over fruit mixture.

- Bake for 24–28 minutes or until topping is deep golden brown and juices are bubbly in center. Serve with Sweetened Whipped Cream or vanilla ice cream, if desired.

Makes 10 to 12 servings.

Lemon Poppyseed Tart with Fresh Berries

To my mind, this tart is meant for teatime, when the tea and lively conversation flow with equal ease.

1	18-ounce roll refrigerated sugar cookie dough, well chilled
2½	tablespoons poppyseeds, divided
2	teaspoons grated lemon zest
1	8-ounce tub whipped cream cheese
1¼	cups jarred lemon curd (or canned lemon pie filling)
2	cups fresh raspberries (or sliced strawberries)

Preheat oven to 350°. Spray a 12-inch pizza pan with nonstick cooking spray.

Crumble cookie dough into a medium bowl; let soften 10–15 minutes. Sprinkle with 2 tablespoons poppyseeds and lemon zest; mix with your fingers or a wooden spoon until combined. With floured fingers, press dough evenly onto the prepared pan to form crust.

Bake 15–19 minutes or until deep golden brown. Cool completely.

Spoon and spread cream cheese to within ½ inch of edge of cookie crust. Spread lemon curd over cream cheese. Arrange berries over lemon curd and sprinkle with remaining ½ tablespoon poppyseeds. Store in refrigerator.

Makes 10 to 12 servings.

Irish Cream Chocolate-Chip Cheesecake Tart

This dessert is for hard-core dessert-aholics—like me. It begins with a thick chocolate-chip cookie base that encloses the richest imaginable filling of Irish cream liqueur, white chocolate, and cream cheese.

1   18-ounce roll refrigerated chocolate-chip cookie dough, well chilled
2   8-ounce packages cream cheese, softened
⅓   cup packed light brown sugar
1   tablespoon all-purpose flour
¼   cup Irish cream liqueur
2   large eggs
1   cup white chocolate chips

• Preheat oven to 350°. Press cookie dough in bottom and 1 inch up sides of an ungreased 10-inch springform pan.

• Bake 10–13 minutes until partially set and light golden brown (crust will appear puffed). Using the back of a metal spoon, gently press dough down against bottom and sides of pan. Cool 15 minutes.

• Meanwhile, in large bowl beat the cream cheese and brown sugar with an electric mixer on high, scraping down sides of the bowl, until smooth. Add flour and liqueur; beat until smooth. Add the eggs, one at a time, beating well after each addition. Stir in white chocolate chips. Pour filling over prepared crust.

• Bake 32–35 minutes or until the edge is set but the center still moves slightly. Cool in the pan on a wire rack for 10 minutes. Loosen the sides of the pan. Cover; refrigerate for at least 3 hours or until completely chilled.

Makes 10 to 12 servings.

Magic Cookie Cupcakes

Some call them magic cookie bars, others know them as 7-layer bars, and still others just know them as the cookie bar at the corner coffee shop they cannot live without. Here they appear as handheld cupcake-style cookies. Don't turn away for too long or they will mysteriously vanish.

1   18-ounce package refrigerated chocolate-chip cookie dough
1   8-ounce package cream cheese, cut into small cubes
2   cups shredded coconut
1   cup graham cracker crumbs
½   cup chopped pecans

Preheat oven to 350°. Line 12 muffin cups with paper baking cups.

Crumble cookie dough into large bowl; add cream cheese and let stand 10 to 15 minutes to soften. Mix with wooden spoon or paddle attachment of an electric mixer until blended. Add coconut, graham cracker crumbs, and pecans. Mix to combine.

Spoon dough evenly into paper-lined cups.

Bake 30–35 minutes or until cookie cups are golden brown and a toothpick inserted in center comes out clean. Cool 5 minutes. Remove from muffin cups. Serve warm or cool.

Makes 12 cookie cupcakes.

Chocolate-Chip Banana Cream Torte

I still remember a birthday party I attended as a child where I was served chocolate-covered frozen bananas as one of an assortment of festive treats—what a winning merger of flavors! Here the same delicious combination is enhanced by a voluptuous layer of pudding and a crown of whipped cream.

1 18-ounce roll refrigerated chocolate-chip cookie dough, well chilled

1 3.4-ounce package banana cream instant pudding and pie filling mix

1¼ cups milk (not nonfat)

2 medium, ripe bananas, sliced

¾ cup heavy whipping cream

½ cup miniature semisweet chocolate chips

Preheat oven to 350°. Spray a 10-inch pie plate with nonstick cooking spray.

Crumble cookie dough into the prepared pan; with floured fingers, press cookie dough onto bottom and up sides of pie plate.

Bake 23–26 minutes or until deep golden brown and firm to the touch at the center; flatten down middle (not sides) with back of spoon to form a shell for the filling. Cool completely on wire rack.

Reserve 1½ tablespoons of the pudding mix. Beat remaining pudding mix and milk with wire whisk or an electric mixer until mixture thickens; refrigerate 5 minutes, until pudding sets up. Spread pudding over cooled cookie crust; top with bananas.

In a small bowl beat whipping cream and reserved pudding mix until stiff peaks form; spread over bananas and sprinkle with miniature chocolate chips. Refrigerate for at least 1 hour or until set.

Makes 8 to 10 servings.

Chocolate-Chip Cookie Dough Cheesecake

In college, I spent the better part of one summer session taking classes at the University of Chicago by day and eating cookie dough ice cream by night. I thought it was one of the best ice cream flavors then, and still think so now. Here I take the same basic idea and transform it into a delectable cheesecake. Good luck limiting yourself to one slice!

1   **18-ounce roll refrigerated chocolate-chip cookie dough, well chilled**
3   **8-ounce packages cream cheese, softened**
⅔   **cup sugar**
1   **teaspoon vanilla extract**
3   **large eggs**
1   **cup miniature semisweet chocolate chips**

Preheat oven to 325°. Press ⅔ of the cookie dough into the bottom of a 10-inch springform pan. Bake 9–11 minutes until partially set and light golden brown (dough will appear slightly puffed).

Meanwhile, in a large bowl combine the cream cheese, sugar, and vanilla. Beat at medium speed with an electric mixer until well blended, stopping periodically to scrape down the sides of the bowl with a rubber spatula.

Add eggs, one at a time, mixing well after each addition and scraping down sides and bottom of the bowl with a rubber spatula. Stir in the chocolate chips and drop ⅔ of the remaining cookie dough by teaspoons into cheesecake batter; fold gently.

Pour batter into crust. Dot with level teaspoons of remaining cookie dough.

Bake 45–50 minutes or until just barely set at the center. Remove from oven. Cool completely on wire rack. Chill in refrigerator at least 4 hours or overnight.

Makes 12 servings.

Special Cookie Dough Treats

Mocha Java Ice Cream-wiches

You may never buy ready-made ice cream sandwiches again. Consider this a template for any cookie–ice cream combination. For example, substitute peanut butter for the fudge sauce, or use sugar cookie dough, jam, and vanilla ice cream for a springtime treat. During the holidays, be on the lookout for gingerbread refrigerated cookie dough. Together with a smear of caramel fudge sauce and eggnog ice cream, it makes a new classic dessert for family and guests.

1   18-ounce roll refrigerated chocolate-chip cookie dough, well chilled
½   cup thick hot fudge ice cream topping
1   pint (2 cups) coffee ice cream, softened

Preheat oven to 350°. Line two 8-inch square pans with foil. Place half of cookie dough in each pan; press in bottoms of pans.

Bake 15–19 minutes or until deep golden brown. Cool completely in pans.

Remove cookies from pans by lifting foil. Invert cookies onto work surface; remove foil. Spread each cookie with fudge topping.

Return foil to one of the pans; place one cookie in the pan, fudge side up. Spread the softened ice cream evenly over fudge topping. Top with remaining cookie, fudge side down. Cover with aluminum foil and place pan in freezer for at least 1 hour or until firm.

Remove cookie sandwich from pan by lifting foil; remove foil. Cut into 12 sandwiches. Tightly wrap each sandwich in a square of aluminum foil. Store in freezer until ready to serve. To serve, let stand at room temperature for 5 minutes before unwrapping.

Makes 12 ice cream sandwiches.

Mandarin Orange & Marmalade Tart

This is a picture-perfect fruit tart that comes together in a flash. The cookie crust can be prepared ahead of time, but don't assemble the tart until the last minute. Otherwise, the moisture from the oranges will make the tart soggy.

1	18-ounce roll refrigerated sugar cookie dough, well chilled
1	cup white chocolate chips
1	8-ounce container soft-spread cheesecake- or honey nut-flavored cream cheese
3	11-ounce cans mandarin orange segments, drained and patted dry
½	cup orange marmalade
	Mint sprigs for garnish (optional)

- Preheat oven to 350°. Spray a 12-inch pizza pan with nonstick cooking spray.

- Cut cookie dough into ¼-inch-thick slices. With floured fingers, press slices evenly onto pan to form crust. Sprinkle with white chocolate chips; gently press chips into dough.

- Bake 15–19 minutes or until deep golden brown. Cool completely.

- Stir cream cheese until of spreading consistency. Spread over crust. Refrigerate at least 30 minutes.

- Just before serving, arrange orange segments on cream cheese layer.

- In a small saucepan over low heat melt the marmalade; brush or spoon over oranges. Garnish with mint sprigs if desired.

Makes 12 servings.

Special Cookie Dough Treats

Chocolate-Chip Berry Trifle

Chocolate-chip cookies and berries snuggled into layers of creamy pudding, then topped with Sweetened Whipped Cream? It's irresistible, and definitely comfort food at its finest.

1   18-ounce roll refrigerated chocolate-chip cookie dough, well chilled
2   cups milk (not nonfat)
2   3.4-ounce packages instant vanilla pudding and pie filling mix
1   3-cup recipe Sweetened Whipped Cream, see page 218
3   cups fresh raspberries (or sliced strawberries)
    Fresh mint leaves for garnish (optional)
    Additional fresh raspberries (or strawberries) for garnish (optional)

- Preheat oven to 375°. Spray cookie sheets with nonstick cooking spray. Cut cookie dough in half lengthwise and then in half again lengthwise, for a total of 4 pieces. Cut cookie dough into 2½-inch logs, ending with 16. Place on prepared cookie sheets.

- Bake 11–13 minutes or until light golden brown and just set at the center. Cool on cookie sheets for 1 minute; remove to wire racks to cool completely.

- In large bowl beat the milk and pudding mix until blended. Set aside. Prepare the Sweetened Whipped Cream. Fold the whipped cream into pudding mixture.

- Crumble 6 cookies. Sprinkle ¾ of the crumbled cookies on bottom of deep 10-inch glass serving dish. Top with ⅓ of pudding mixture. Distribute berries over pudding. Stand remaining 10 cookies, face side out, along the inside of dish. Place remaining pudding mixture over berries. Top with remaining crushed cookies.

- Cover trifle; refrigerate for 4 hours or overnight. Garnish with mint leaves and berries, if desired.

Special Cookie Dough Treats   *Makes 10 to 12 servings.*

Summer Fruit & Lemon Curd Pizza Tart

On a quest for the perfect dessert for a summer barbecue? Look no further.

1	18-ounce roll refrigerated sugar cookie dough, well chilled
¼	cup seedless raspberry jam, melted
¾	cup prepared lemon curd
2	cups fresh raspberries
1	cup fresh blackberries
1	cup hulled, sliced strawberries
3	kiwi, peeled and sliced
2	teaspoons sugar

• Preheat oven to 350°. Spray a 12-inch pizza pan with nonstick cooking spray.

• Cut cookie dough into ¼-inch-thick slices. With floured fingers, press slices evenly onto pan to form crust.

• Bake 15–19 minutes or until deep golden brown. Cool completely.

• Preheat broiler. Spread jam over crust. Spread lemon curd over jam; arrange raspberries, blackberries, strawberry slices, and kiwi slices on top. Sprinkle sugar over fruit; broil 3 minutes. Cut into wedges and serve.

Baker's Note: For an extra-fancy finish, drizzle top of finished tart with 1 recipe Chocolate Dip/Drizzle (see page 201). Use either white or semisweet chocolate.

Makes 8 to 10 servings.

Special Cookie Dough Treats

Gingered Nectarine & Mascarpone Tart

This tart is idyllic summer dessert fare. Moreover, it comes together quickly since nectarines rarely need peeling. The mascarpone filling is a breeze as well. Mascarpone is a fresh, Italian dessert cheese with a delicate flavor and velvety texture. Look for it in the imported cheese section of the supermarket. In a pinch, substitute two 8-ounce packages of cream cheese, softened, for the mascarpone.

1	18-ounce roll refrigerated sugar cookie dough, well chilled
2	8-ounce containers mascarpone cheese (Italian cream cheese)
¼	cup sugar
1	tablespoon grated lemon zest
¼	teaspoon vanilla extract
3	tablespoons finely chopped crystallized ginger, divided
5	or 6 small nectarines, halved, pitted, cut into thin slices
⅓	cup peach jam, warmed
	Fresh mint sprigs for garnish (optional)

●Preheat oven to 350°. Spray a 12-inch pizza pan with nonstick cooking spray.

●Cut cookie dough into ¼-inch-thick slices. With floured fingers, press slices evenly onto pan to form crust.

●Bake 15–19 minutes or until deep golden brown. Cool completely.

●In medium bowl beat the mascarpone, sugar, lemon zest, and vanilla until smooth. Beat in 1 tablespoon crystallized ginger. Spread filling over prepared crust. Cover loosely and refrigerate at least 2 hours or up to 1 day.

●Overlap nectarine slices atop filling in concentric circles.

●In a small saucepan over low heat melt the peach jam. Brush melted jam over nectarine slices; sprinkle with remaining chopped crystallized ginger and garnish with mint sprigs, if desired. Serve or refrigerate up to 6 hours.

Makes 8 to 10 servings.

Taffy-Toffee Caramel Apple Tart

This tastes like biting into a perfect caramel apple, with the added bonus of crunchy sugar cookie in every bite. You won't taste peanut butter in the creamy filling layer, just a smooth taffy-toffee layer that complements the apples.

1	18-ounce roll refrigerated sugar cookie dough, well chilled
1	8-ounce package cream cheese, softened
⅓	cup peanut butter
¼	cup packed brown sugar
1	teaspoon vanilla extract
¼	teaspoon ground cinnamon
2	large Granny Smith (or Golden Delicious) apples, peeled, cored, and very thinly sliced
2	to 3 teaspoons lemon juice (optional)
⅓	cup caramel apple dip (or thick caramel ice cream topping)
½	cup toffee baking bits (or sliced almonds)

- Preheat oven to 350°. Spray a 12-inch pizza pan with nonstick cooking spray.

- Cut cookie dough into ¼-inch-thick slices. With floured fingers, press slices evenly onto pan to form crust.

- Bake 15–19 minutes or until deep golden brown. Cool completely.

- In a medium mixing bowl beat cream cheese, peanut butter, brown sugar, vanilla, and cinnamon with an electric mixer on medium speed until combined. Spread mixture evenly over the cooled crust.

- Sprinkle apple slices with lemon juice to prevent browning, if desired. Arrange apple slices atop cream cheese mixture; drizzle with caramel topping. Sprinkle with almonds or toffee bits. Cut into wedges to serve.

Makes 10 to 12 servings.

Baker's Note: To make tart ahead of time, prepare crust as above; spread cream cheese mixture topping on cooled crust. Cover and refrigerate up to 24 hours. Top with apple slices and continue final preparation as directed above.

Special Cookie Dough Treats

Blueberry Cookie Pie

This yummy, fruity pie is made for long summer days when the weather is warm, the days are dappled in sunshine, and blueberries are at their peak. But if a longing for blueberries strikes in the dead of winter, hope is alive: this recipe is equally delicious made with frozen blueberries.

1   18-ounce roll refrigerated sugar cookie dough, well chilled
⅓   cup all-purpose flour
3   cups fresh (or frozen) blueberries, thawed if using frozen berries
¾   cup sugar
3   tablespoons cornstarch
    Dash salt
1   teaspoon lemon juice

- Preheat oven to 350°. Spray a 9-inch pie pan and small cookie sheet with nonstick cooking spray.

- In a medium bowl, combine sugar cookie dough and flour with your fingers, paddle attachment of an electric mixer, or wooden spoon until combined. Remove ¼ of the cookie dough; cover with plastic wrap and refrigerate.

- With floured fingers, press remaining dough into bottom and sides of the prepared pie pan. Place in the freezer about 15 minutes.

- On a lightly floured surface, roll reserved dough to ¼-inch thickness. Use small cookie cutters to cut out shapes. Place cut-outs on the prepared cookie sheet.

- Bake cookie dough piecrust for about 13–15 minutes or until deep golden brown; place on wire rack and cool completely.

- Bake cookie cutouts for about 6 minutes. Remove to wire racks; cool completely.

Special Cookie Dough Treats

In a medium saucepan combine 1 cup blueberries, sugar, cornstarch, and salt. Stir in ⅔ cup water and the lemon juice. Bring to boil, stirring constantly until mixture thickens, crushing blueberries while stirring. Stir in remaining blueberries, remove from heat and cool completely. Spoon blueberry mixture into cooled cookie shell; top with cookie cutouts. Chill at least 1 hour.

Makes 8 servings.

Special Cookie Dough Treats

Blueberry Cookie Pie

Strawberry Ice Cream Sundae Birthday Tart

This is one of those showstopper birthday desserts that turns a party into a full-fledged celebration. Strawberry ice cream (my recommendation, but you can substitute vanilla or chocolate) is embellished with fresh berries, berry sauce, and toasted coconut, making more than enough to feed a crowd.

2	pints strawberry ice cream
1	18-ounce roll refrigerated sugar cookie dough, well chilled
½	cup sliced almonds
1	tablespoon sugar
¼	teaspoon ground cinnamon
4	cups sliced fresh strawberries, chilled
¾	cup strawberry ice cream topping
1	cup lightly toasted shredded coconut

- Use an ice cream scoop to form 12 balls of ice cream. Place the ice cream balls on a large cold plate; cover and store in the freezer.

- Preheat oven to 350°. Line an 11 x 7 x 1½-inch baking pan with foil. Coat foil lightly with cooking spray.

- Cut cookie dough into ¼-inch-thick slices. With floured fingers, press slices evenly onto pan to form crust. Sprinkle the almonds over the cookie dough; press almonds lightly into dough. In a small bowl stir together the sugar and cinnamon. Using a teaspoon, sprinkle mixture over dough.

- Bake 18–22 minutes or until deep golden brown. Cool completely. Carefully remove crust from pan, using the foil to lift it. Gently peel foil from crust. Carefully place crust on serving tray.

•Just before serving, stir strawberries into ice cream topping. Quickly transfer ice cream scoops from freezer to crust. Spoon some of the strawberry mixture on top. Sprinkle with toasted coconut. Cut tart into 12 pieces. Serve immediately. Pass remaining strawberry mixture to spoon on top of each serving.

Baker's Note: Scoop ice cream balls up to 48 hours ahead of time. Prepare crust; cool, cover, and let stand up to 1 day before using.

Makes 12 servings.

Deep-Dish Heath Bar Cheesecake Pie

This decadent cookie cheesecake is sinful before you add the toffee bits and to-die-for once you do. It is so rich it doesn't need a garnish. On the other hand, for a complete dessert blowout, warm some chocolate fudge or caramel ice cream topping, drizzle over each slice, and dollop with whipped cream.

1	18-ounce roll refrigerated chocolate-chip cookie dough, well chilled
2	8-ounce packages cream cheese, softened
½	cup sugar
1	teaspoon vanilla extract
2	large eggs
4	(1.4-ounce) Heath or other chocolate-covered English toffee candy bars, coarsely chopped

• Preheat oven to 350°. Coat a 9- or 10-inch deep-dish pie pan with nonstick cooking spray.

• Slice cookie dough into ¼-inch-slices and arrange on the bottom and up the sides of the pie plate. With floured fingers, press dough together to form crust; set aside.

• In a large bowl beat the cream cheese, sugar, and vanilla for 1 minute with an electric mixer on medium speed. Stop mixer and scrape down sides of bowl with rubber spatula. Beat 1 minute longer.

• Add eggs, one at a time, beating until just blended. Stir in the chopped toffee; pour into the pie plate.

• Bake 38–42 minutes or until the center is just set. Cool completely. Cover loosely, then chill for at least 4 hours or overnight before serving.

Makes 8 to 10 servings.

Special Cookie Dough Treats

Tropical Fruit Pizza Tart

This showy fruit tart has much to offer—a crisp cookie base, four varieties of tropical fruit, a layer of creamy lime cream cheese, and an easy apricot glaze.

- 1 18-ounce roll refrigerated sugar cookie dough, well chilled
- ⅓ cup sugar
  Juice and grated zest of 1 small lime
- 1 8-ounce package cream cheese, softened
- 1 cup diced, peeled ripe mango
- 1 large banana, peeled and sliced
  6 ½-inch slices fresh pineapple, cut in half
- 2 kiwi, each peeled and cut into 8 slices
- ⅓ cup apricot preserves
- ⅓ cup lightly toasted shredded coconut

- Preheat oven to 350°. Spray a 12-inch pizza pan with nonstick cooking spray.

- Cut cookie dough into ¼-inch-thick slices. With floured fingers, press slices evenly onto pan to form crust.

- Bake 15–19 minutes or until deep golden brown. Cool completely.

- In a medium bowl combine the sugar, lime juice, lime zest, and cream cheese; beat with an electric mixer at medium speed until smooth. Spread cream cheese mixture over cookie crust, leaving a ½-inch margin around edges.

- Arrange mango, banana, pineapple, and kiwi on top of cream cheese mixture in a decorative pattern.

- In a small saucepan set over low heat melt the apricot preserves, stirring until just melted. Drizzle or brush over fruit; sprinkle with toasted coconut. Chill 1 hour before serving.

Makes 8 to 10 servings.

Special Cookie Dough Treats

Tropical Fruit Pizza Tart

Cookie Tiramisu

Tiramisu has become a new standard on American dessert menus. Now you can make a simple variation of this favorite concoction with familiar ingredients from your refrigerator and pantry.

1	18-ounce roll refrigerated sugar cookie dough, well chilled
1	8-ounce package cream cheese, softened
¼	cup sugar
¾	cup strong coffee, cooled, divided
1	tablespoon rum (or coffee liqueur)
1	2-cup recipe Sweetened Whipped Cream, see page 218
1	tablespoon unsweetened cocoa

Preheat oven to 350°. Spray cookie sheets with nonstick cooking spray.

Cut cookie dough into 20 equal pieces. Shape into 2½ x 1-inch oblong shapes. Place on prepared sheets.

Bake 10–12 minutes or until light golden brown around edges. Cool on cookie sheets for 1 minute. Remove to wire racks and cool completely.

In a large mixing bowl beat the cream cheese and sugar with an electric mixer on high speed until smooth. Beat in ¼ cup cooled coffee and rum or liqueur. Fold in Sweetened Whipped Cream.

Layer 6 cookies in 8-inch-square baking dish. Sprinkle each cookie with ⅓ of remaining coffee. Spread ⅓ of the cream cheese mixture over cookies. Repeat layers two more times with 12 cookies, remaining coffee, and remaining cream cheese mixture.

Cover tiramisu and refrigerate 2–3 hours. Crumble remaining 2 cookies over top. Sift cocoa over cookies. Cut into squares.

Makes 8 servings.

Candy Shop Cookie Tart

This indulgent cookie tart is all of my childhood candy fantasies pulled together into one irresistible confection. Be as creative as you like—restraint does not suit this decadent dessert.

- 1   18-ounce roll refrigerated sugar cookie dough, well chilled
- 1   cup semi-sweet chocolate chips
- ½   cup creamy or chunky peanut butter
- 2   cups (about 5 candy bars) coarsely chopped assorted chocolate candy bars

- Preheat oven to 350°. Spray a 12-inch pizza pan with nonstick cooking spray.

- Cut cookie dough into ¼-inch-thick slices. With floured fingers, press slices evenly onto pan to form crust.

- Bake 15–19 minutes or until deep golden brown. Remove from oven and immediately sprinkle chocolate chips over hot crust; drop peanut butter by spoonfuls onto morsels. Let stand for 5 minutes or until morsels are shiny. Gently spread chocolate and peanut butter evenly over cookie crust.

- Sprinkle candy in single layer over pizza pan. Cut into wedges; serve warm or at room temperature.

Baker's Note: Chocolate-chip cookie dough can be used in place of the sugar cookie dough.

Makes 10 to 12 servings.

Special Cookie Dough Treats

Pear & Raspberry Frangipane Tart

This wonderful tart combines pears and raspberries in sophisticated harmony. Frangipane is a rich, but easy to prepare, pastry cream flavored with ground almonds and used to fill or top pastries and cakes. The history of the name is equally rich. In the sixteenth century an Italian nobleman, Marquis Muzio Frangipani, created a perfume for scenting gloves with a slightly almond aroma. Its esteem in Paris was so high that pastry chefs created an almond-flavored pastry cream in its honor and christened it "frangipane."

1	18-ounce roll refrigerated sugar cookie dough, well chilled
3	tablespoons seedless raspberry jam
1	cup whole blanched almonds
¼	cup butter
½	cup sugar
1	tablespoon all-purpose flour
1	large egg
1	teaspoon almond extract
1	15½-ounce can sliced pears

• Preheat oven to 350°. Press dough in bottom and up sides of ungreased 10-inch springform pan. Spread jam evenly over bottom.

• Place almonds in food processor bowl with metal blade or blender container; process until finely chopped. Add butter, sugar, and flour; process until blended. Add egg and almond extract; process until blended.

• Drain pears, reserving ¼ cup liquid. Add reserved liquid to almond mixture; blend until smooth. Spread almond filling evenly in crust. Arrange pear slices over filling.

• Bake 40–45 minutes or until crust is lightly browned and top is deep golden brown. Cool completely.

Makes 8 to 10 servings.

Special Cookie Dough Treats

Raspberry Chocolate Cookie Tart

The always enticing combination of raspberries and chocolate in this showstopper tart is well worth the mild effort required to make it.

1   18-ounce roll refrigerated chocolate-chip cookie dough, well chilled
1   8-ounce package cream cheese, softened
¼   cup sifted powdered sugar
1   tablespoon fresh orange juice
1   teaspoon grated orange zest
2   cups fresh raspberries
¼   cup semi-sweet chocolate chips
¼   teaspoon vegetable oil

Preheat oven to 350°. Spray a 12-inch pizza pan with nonstick cooking spray.

Cut cookie dough into ¼-inch-thick slices. With floured fingers, press slices evenly onto pan to form crust.

Bake 15–19 minutes or until deep golden brown. Cool completely.

In a medium bowl combine the cream cheese, powdered sugar, orange juice, and orange zest; beat with an electric mixer on medium speed until well blended. Spread over cooled crust. Arrange raspberries over cream cheese.

In small saucepan over low heat melt the chocolate chips with vegetable oil, stirring until smooth; drizzle over raspberries. Let stand at least 30 minutes or until chocolate is set before serving.

Makes 10 to 12 servings.

Special Cookie Dough Treats

Deep-Dish Chocolate-Chip Pecan Pie

You can savor this chocoholic version of pecan pie year-round, but it is supremely suited for celebrating during the holidays. This pie pleases everyone, under every circumstance. If you want, serve slices with an extra drizzle of warmed fudge sauce and vanilla ice cream or whipped cream— New Year's resolutions can wait.

1	18-ounce roll refrigerated chocolate-chip cookie dough, well chilled
½	cup firmly packed brown sugar
⅓	cup unsweetened cocoa
1	cup dark corn syrup
1½	teaspoons vanilla extract
2	large eggs
1	cup coarsely chopped pecans

Preheat oven to 350°. Cut cookie dough into ¼-inch-thick slices. Press cookie dough in bottom and 1 inch up sides of 10-inch springform pan; set aside.

In a large bowl combine the brown sugar and cocoa; mix well. Add corn syrup, vanilla, and eggs; whisk until smooth. Stir in pecans. Pour mixture into crust.

Bake 40–44 minutes or until center is puffed and knife inserted in center comes out clean. Cool completely. Serve at room temperature or refrigerate until serving time.

Makes 8 to 10 servings.

Apricot Amaretto Cookie Tart

In my mind, canned apricots are one of the best canned items on the market. Together with the flavor of almonds—sliced and in the amaretto—this tart looks and tastes like a selection from a premiere pastry shop.

1	18-ounce roll refrigerated sugar cookie dough, well chilled
1	8-ounce package cream cheese, softened
¼	cup sugar
3	tablespoons amaretto, divided
2	large eggs
2	tablespoons apricot preserves
1	15-ounce can apricot halves, well drained
½	cup sliced almonds
	Fresh mint sprigs (optional)

Preheat oven to 350°. Cut cookie dough into ¼-inch-thick slices. Press cookie dough in bottom and 1 inch up sides of 10-inch springform pan; set aside.

In a medium bowl beat the cream cheese and sugar with an electric mixer until light and fluffy, stopping once or twice to scrape down the sides of the bowl with a rubber spatula. Add 2 tablespoons amaretto and eggs; beat until smooth. Pour filling into prepared crust.

Bake 36–40 minutes or until filling is just set. Cool completely. Refrigerate at least 2 hours or until completely chilled.

Just before serving, in a medium bowl combine the apricot preserves and 1 tablespoon amaretto; mix well. Add apricots; stir to coat. Arrange apricot halves, rounded side up over top of tart. Garnish with mint sprigs, if desired. Store in refrigerator.

Makes 10 to 12 servings.

Special Cookie Dough Treats

6 Icings, Frostings, and Other Adornments

Since cookie dough cookies can be so quick to make, why not put some of that extra time toward some edible embellishments. With as little as a few candies, sprinkles, or chocolate drizzle, you can change an already yummy cookie into a showstopper in a matter of minutes.

And if you think frostings and icings are for cakes, think again. What follows are minimalist recipes: few ingredients and little fuss. "Less is more" was my guiding principle, so expect perfect results and big flavor with every recipe, every time.

Each recipe is enough to frost one batch of cookies made with an 18-ounce roll of refrigerated cookie dough.

A Few Decorating Ideas

Adding Color to Your Cookies

You don't have to be an artist to change cookies into miniature masterpieces. With a careful hand, an array of colors can be used to add a designer touch to refrigerated cookie dough. Use one or more of the following suggestions to tint either icing (such as decorating icing and cookie frosting at the beginning of this chapter) or the cookie dough itself (sugar cookie dough, only—I don't think the world is quite ready for purple and green chocolate-chip cookies!).

What follows is a summary of some readily available products available for these purposes:

Liquid Food Coloring: This is the easiest to find and least expensive food coloring, available in four basic colors—blue, red, yellow, and green. You can buy a package with a small bottle of each color or purchase larger bottles of single colors. Use this for mixing pastel shades only. To make vibrant colors you would need to add enough color to liquefy the icing, making it too thin to use. Do not use liquid coloring to tint melted white chocolate or candy coating because it will cause graininess or clumping.

Liquid Paste: Thicker than liquid, these colors come in about 20 hues and dispense drop by drop with little mess. Liquid paste colors mix easily and create vivid colors.

Paste: Dozens of shades of paste colors are available packed individually or in sets. Use them to achieve intense and dark colors. Paste color works particularly well in frostings and dough for cutout cookies because it doesn't thin them. Use only paste to tint melted white chocolate and candy coating.

Powder: Brush powder color on white or pastel frosting with a dry brush to create shading. You'll find a wide range of colors available. Powder color can be used to tint dry ingredients such as granulated or powdered sugars, but cannot be used to tint cookie dough.

Most supermarkets carry liquid colors. For other types of food coloring, you may need to go to a specialty or cake and candy supply store. Food colors also are available from specialty mail-order catalogs. Store all colors tightly sealed in a cool place.

Other Decorating Options

It does not necessarily take frosting, icing, or cookie painting to give a cookie that special finishing touch—just some imagination. What follows is a slew of other quick and easy options, from cutters to candies to ribbons. Let your creative side take hold and have fun developing your own unique cookie style.

Cookie Cutters: If you think cookie cutters are limited to hearts, circles, and Christmas trees, take a look in the baking section of your local cooking supply store or check out some of the sources located in the appendix on page 223. The options are far-ranging: specialty wedding cutters, letters, names, dogs (by breed), fruits, vegetables, and just about every other shape you can imagine. Limit your cookie rolling to the sugar cookie dough; chocolate-chip dough does not roll well and will not hold the shape of the cutters once baked (see Basic Rolled Sugar Cookies on page 62).

Sprinkles: An easy way to give sparkle to cookies is to sprinkle them with pearl or coarse sugar or edible glitter. Check out mail-order options (see page 223) or shops that specialize in cake-decorating supplies for other products. Look for additional decorative items such as petal dust (a powdered food coloring that may be brushed on cookies or frosting) and nonpareils (tiny sugar balls).

Icings, Frostings, & Other Adornments

Candyland Trims: Nothing's easier—or sweeter—than a quick candy trim. Most candies melt if placed on cookies before baking, so it's best to arrange candy pieces on frosted cookies. Try sliced gumdrops and red cinnamon candy to make bells or holly and berries, or crushed peppermint for a cool and colorful finish. Here's a short list of candy and other easy toppers ideas:

- Cinnamon "Red Hots"
- Chocolate coffee beans and chocolate-covered espresso beans
- Chocolate-covered mints (e.g., Junior Mints)
- Life Savers
- Chopped candy bars (e.g., chocolate-covered toffee bars)
- Small-size jelly beans
- Licorice
- Gummy bears
- Gum drops
- Necco wafers
- Candied almonds
- Raisins, dried cranberries, and other dried fruit chopped into small pieces
- Candied and glacé cherries and fruits

Chocolate

Cookies drizzled or coated with chocolate are dressed for any occasion. Use a spoon to drizzle melted chocolate over the cookies or dip half of each cookie into melted chocolate. Garnish frosted bars with grated chocolate or chocolate curls.

Chocolate Drizzle or Dip

1 cup semi-sweet, milk chocolate, or white chocolate chips
1 tablespoon vegetable shortening

- In a small heavy saucepan over low heat melt the chips and shortening, stirring often to avoid scorching.

Chocolate Drizzle

- Place cookies on a wire rack over waxed paper. Dip a fork or knife into melted chocolate and let the first clumpy drip land back in the pan. Then drizzle the chocolate over the edge of the pan onto the cookies. Let the cookies stand until the chocolate is set.

- Makes enough to dip or drizzle one batch of refrigerated cookie dough cookies.

Chocolate Dip

- Dip a cookie into the mixture. Remove the excess chocolate by pulling the cookie across the edge of the pan.

No-Prep Frostings or Sandwich Cookie Fillings

Sometimes the best "recipes" require no work at all. This short list of no-prep frostings can change your chocolate-chip or sugar cookies into masterpieces in minutes. Sandwich chocolate-chip cookies around a thin or thick dollop of peanut butter or chocolate-hazelnut spread; squeeze squiggles, dots, and doodles with tubes of decorating icing; or spread sugar cookies with strawberry-flavored cream cheese for instant cheesecake cookies.

- Peanut Butter
- Peanut Butter & Jelly
- Soft-Spread Sweetened Cream Cheese
- Chocolate hazelnut spread (e.g., Nutella)
- Jam or preserves
- Jarred lemon curd
- Canned cake frosting
- Marshmallow creme

Cookie Decorating Icing

Egg whites act as a stabilizer in this icing, allowing it to harden for decorating the cookies. Because the whites are not cooked, I prefer to use powdered egg whites (e.g., Just Whites). They are available in the baking section of most supermarkets.

- **1   16-ounce box powdered sugar**
- **4   teaspoons powdered egg whites (not reconstituted)**
- **⅓   cup water**
- **1   tablespoon fresh lemon juice**
- **1   teaspoon vanilla extract**
- **Food coloring (optional)**

Beat together all ingredients except food coloring in a large bowl with an electric mixer at moderate speed until just combined, about 1 minute. Increase speed to high and beat icing, scraping down side of bowl occasionally, until it holds stiff peaks, about 3 minutes in standing mixer or 4–5 minutes with a handheld.

Beat in food coloring, if desired. If you plan to spread (rather than pipe) icing on cookies, stir in more water, 1 teaspoon at a time, to thin to desired consistency.

Baker's Note: For a two-color icing variation, spread one color of icing evenly over a baked sliced cookie or cookie cutout. While the first color is still wet, apply dots or lines of a second color of icing. Use a toothpick to pull through the dots or lines, making a design or giving a marbled look.

Makes about 3 cups.

Sugar Cookie Paint

Cookie paint is essentially a colored egg wash. Paint it onto slices of refrigerated sugar cookie dough before baking to produce shiny cookies with brilliant colors and a glossy sheen. This is a wonderful rainy-day activity for children as well as a fun party break for adults. Use small artist brushes—made with natural bristles—to apply the paint and let your inner artist break free!

1   **large egg yolk**
⅛   **teaspoon water**
    Liquid paste (or powder) food coloring of choice

- In a small bowl combine the egg yolk and water. Add a dab or two of coloring if using paste, a pinch if using powder; mix well.
- Use an artist's brush to apply the paint to the cookies before baking.

Makes enough for one batch of cookies.

Fresh Citrus (Lemon, Lime, or Orange) Icing

1½ **cups sifted powdered sugar**
1   **teaspoon grated lemon, lime, or orange zest**
2½ **to 3 tablespoons fresh lemon, lime, or orange juice**

- Place powered sugar in medium bowl. Mix in zest and enough juice as needed to make icing just thin enough to drip off fork.

Makes about ¾ cup.

Maple Icing

- ¼ cup (½ stick) butter, softened
- 2¼ cups sifted powdered sugar
- 1 teaspoon maple-flavored extract
- 3 to 4 teaspoons milk

In a medium bowl cream butter with an electric mixer or a wooden spoon; gradually add powdered sugar. Stir in maple extract and enough milk to make frosting of spreading consistency.

Makes about ¾ cup.

Almond Icing

- 3 tablespoons hot water
- 1½ teaspoons almond extract
- Pinch of salt
- 2¾ cups powdered sugar

In a small bowl mix water, almond extract, and salt. Whisk in enough powdered sugar to form frosting thick enough to pipe or spread.

Makes about 1 cup.

Easy Cocoa Icing

5   tablespoons unsalted butter, softened
2   cups sifted powdered sugar, divided
2   to 4 tablespoons milk
¾   teaspoon vanilla extract
½   cup unsweetened cocoa powder

In a large bowl beat the butter until fluffy. Gradually beat in 1 cup powered sugar. Beat in 1 tablespoon milk and vanilla. Add cocoa and remaining sugar; beat until blended, thinning with more milk if necessary.

Makes about 1⅓ cups.

Vanilla Butter Frosting

¼   cup (½ stick) butter, softened
2   cups sifted powdered sugar
1   teaspoon vanilla extract
1   to 1½ tablespoons milk

In a large bowl cream the butter with an electric mixer or a wooden spoon; gradually add powdered sugar. Stir in vanilla extract and enough milk to make icing of spreading consistency.

Makes about ¾ cup.

Peanut Butter Icing

- 6 tablespoons creamy-style peanut butter
- 1½ cups sifted powdered sugar
- 1½ tablespoons milk

In a medium mixing bowl combine the peanut butter, powdered sugar, and milk. Beat with electric mixer on medium-high speed until combined and smooth. Add more milk, by the teaspoon, if needed to make icing drizzling consistency.

Makes about ¾ cup.

Apricot Frosting

- 1½ cups sifted powdered sugar
- 1½ tablespoons butter, softened
- 6 tablespoons apricot preserves

Combine all ingredients in a small mixing bowl. Beat at medium speed with an electric mixer until smooth.

Makes about ¾ cup.

Caramel Frosting

6 tablespoons butter
¾ cup packed dark brown sugar
3 tablespoons milk
1½ cups sifted powdered sugar

In a medium saucepan set over medium heat melt the butter; stir in brown sugar. Heat butter mixture to boiling, stirring constantly. Remove from heat and stir in milk.

Gradually stir powdered sugar into butter mixture, beating with spoon until spreadable consistency. If frosting is too thick add milk, a few drops at a time, to thin.

Makes about 1¼ cups.

Cream Cheese Frosting

6 ounces cream cheese, softened
¼ cup (½ stick) unsalted butter, softened
1 teaspoon vanilla extract
1¾ cups sifted powdered sugar

In a medium bowl beat the cream cheese, butter, and vanilla with an electric mixer until smooth. Add powdered sugar and beat until smooth.

Makes about 1⅓ cups.

Bourbon Frosting

- 3 tablespoons butter, softened
- 1½ cups sifted powdered sugar
- 1 tablespoon bourbon
- 1 tablespoon milk

•Place the butter in a medium mixing bowl and beat with an electric mixer until creamy. Gradually add powdered sugar, bourbon, and milk, beating until spreading consistency.

Makes about 1 cup.

Chocolate Cream Cheese Frosting

- ⅔ cup semi-sweet chocolate chips
- 2 tablespoons heavy whipping cream
- 1 3-ounce package cream cheese
- ¼ cup sifted powdered sugar

•In a double boiler melt the chips and add heavy cream. Mix until smooth. Remove from heat.

•In a medium mixing bowl beat the cream cheese and sugar with an electric mixer until smooth. Slowly add chocolate mixture, beating until smooth. Mixture will thicken as the chocolate cools.

Makes about 1 cup.

Lady Baltimore Frosting

½ cup golden raisins, chopped
½ cup chopped dried figs (about 8 whole, stems removed)
1 tablespoon brandy (or bourbon)
3 tablespoons chopped red or green candied cherries
1 cup canned creamy white cake frosting

Place chopped raisins and figs in a small bowl. Stir in brandy; let stand 30 minutes (do not drain). Stir together the brandy-fruit mixture, candied cherries, and white frosting.

Makes about 1½ cups.

Butter-Rum Icing

2 cups sifted powdered sugar
¼ cup (½ stick) butter, melted
2½ teaspoons rum extract, divided
2 to 3 tablespoons milk

In a small bowl combine the powdered sugar, butter, and rum extract. Add just enough milk to make icing of spreading consistency.

Makes about ¾ cup.

Dark Chocolate Frosting

3   tablespoons butter (or margarine)
2   tablespoons corn syrup
2   tablespoons water
2   ounces unsweetened baking chocolate, chopped
2   teaspoons vanilla
¾   to 1 cup sifted powdered sugar

In a medium saucepan set over medium-high heat combine the butter, corn syrup, and water; bring to a boil. Remove from heat. Stir in chocolate, whisking until melted. With wire whisk beat in vanilla and enough powdered sugar until frosting is of spreading consistency.

Makes about ¾ cup.

Peanut Butter & Honey Frosting

¼   cup creamy-style peanut butter
2   tablespoons honey
2   tablespoons hot water
1½ cups sifted powdered sugar

In a medium bowl combine the peanut butter, honey, and hot water with a wooden spoon until smooth. Stir in powdered sugar, adding a few more drops of hot water if needed to make icing spreading consistency.

Makes about ¾ cup.

Browned Butter Frosting

3 tablespoons butter
1½ cups sifted powdered sugar
1 teaspoon vanilla extract
2 to 4 teaspoons milk

In a medium saucepan set over medium heat melt the butter until light brown in color (watch butter carefully—it can burn quickly). Remove from heat.

Stir in the powdered sugar, vanilla, and 1 tablespoon milk into browned butter. Stir in just enough more milk to make frosting smooth and spreadable. Stir in more milk if mixture is too thick or more powdered sugar if mixture is too thin.

Rum Variation: Substitute rum-flavored extract for vanilla extract.

Maple Variation: Substitute maple-flavored extract for vanilla extract.

Coffee Variation: Prepare as above adding 2 teaspoons instant coffee powder or espresso powder along with powdered sugar.

Baker's Note: Be sure to use real butter, not margarine, for this recipe. Margarine will not brown and get the nutty flavor that butter will.

Makes about ¾ cup.

Chocolate Ganache Frosting

⅔ cup heavy whipping cream
6   ounces semi-sweet baking chocolate, chopped

Heat the cream in a medium, heavy-bottomed saucepan over low heat until cream is hot but not boiling; remove from heat.

Stir chopped chocolate into hot cream; stir until melted and smooth. Let stand five minutes. The ganache is ready to use when it mounds slightly when dropped from a spoon. The ganache becomes firmer as it cools.

Makes about 1¼ cups.

Peppermint Icing

1¾ cups sifted powdered sugar
2   tablespoons butter, softened
¼   teaspoon peppermint extract
3   to 4 teaspoons milk (or cream)

In a small bowl stir together the powdered sugar, softened butter, peppermint extract, and enough of the milk or cream to make icing that is easy to drizzle.

Makes about ¾ cup.

Creamy Chocolate Cookie Frosting

- 2 cups sifted powdered sugar
- ¼ cup (½ stick) butter, softened
- 1¼ teaspoons vanilla extract
- 2 1-ounce squares unsweetened baking chocolate, melted and cooled
- 2 to 3 tablespoons milk

In a medium bowl mix the powdered sugar and butter with a wooden spoon or an electric mixer on low speed. Stir in vanilla and chocolate. Gradually beat in just enough milk to make frosting smooth and spreadable. Add more milk as necessary to make spreadable, or more powdered sugar if mixture becomes too thin.

Mocha Variation: Add 2½ teaspoons instant espresso or coffee powder along with powdered sugar.

White Chocolate Variation: Substitute 2 ounces chopped white chocolate baking bar, melted and cooled, for the semi-sweet chocolate.

Makes about 1½ cups.

White Chocolate Cream Cheese Frosting

- 1 cup white chocolate chips
- 6 ounces cream cheese, room temperature
- 2 tablespoons unsalted butter, room temperature
- 1 tablespoon fresh lemon juice

Stir white chocolate in top of double boiler over barely simmering water until almost melted. Remove from over water and stir until smooth. Cool to lukewarm. In a large bowl beat the cream cheese and butter until blended. Beat in lemon juice, then cooled white chocolate.

Makes about 1¼ cups.

Milk Chocolate Sour Cream Frosting

- 1 cup milk chocolate chips
- ⅓ cup sour cream
- 1 teaspoon vanilla extract

Melt chocolate in a double boiler or a large metal bowl over a saucepan of simmering water, stirring occasionally. Remove bowl from heat, then whisk in sour cream and vanilla. Cool to room temperature, stirring occasionally (frosting will become thick enough to spread). Use immediately to frost cookies.

Makes about 1¼ cups.

Chocolate Raspberry Frosting

- 6 ounces semi-sweet chocolate, chopped
- ½ cup sour cream
- 4 tablespoons seedless raspberry jam
- 1½ tablespoons light corn syrup
- 1 teaspoon vanilla extract
- 1½ tablespoons unsalted butter, room temperature

Stir chocolate in top of double boiler over simmering water until melted and smooth. Pour chocolate into large bowl. Cool to room temperature. Add sour cream, jam, corn syrup, and vanilla to chocolate. Using an electric mixer, beat until mixture is fluffy, smooth and light in color, about 3 minutes. Beat in butter.

Makes about 1¼ cups.

Icings, Frostings, & Other Adornments

Coconut Pecan Frosting

½   of a 5-ounce can evaporated milk
¼   cup (½ stick) unsalted butter, softened
¼   cup sugar
1   large egg yolk, beaten to blend
1½ teaspoons all-purpose flour
½   teaspoon vanilla extract
¾   cup chopped pecans
¾   cup flaked sweetened coconut

In a heavy large saucepan combine the evaporated milk, butter, sugar, egg yolk, flour, and vanilla. Whisk constantly over medium-low heat until butter melts and mixture thickens (do not boil), about 10 minutes. Stir in pecans and coconut. Cool until frosting is thick enough to spread but is still warm, about 40 minutes. Generously spread warm frosting onto cookies.

Makes about 1⅓ cups.

Irish Cream Frosting

½   cup (1 stick) unsalted butter, softened
1½ cups powdered sugar, sifted
    Pinch of salt
3½ tablespoons Irish cream liqueur

In a medium bowl cream the butter with an electric mixer until it is smooth. Beat in the powdered sugar, gradually; beat in the salt and the Irish cream. Beat the frosting until it is light and fluffy.

Makes about 1¼ cups.

Marmalade Cream Cheese Frosting

1   8-ounce package cream cheese, softened
¾   cup sifted powdered sugar
⅓   cup orange marmalade
3   tablespoons unsalted butter, softened
1   teaspoon grated orange peel (optional)

• Using an electric mixer, beat cream cheese and sugar in large bowl until smooth. Add marmalade, butter, and orange peel and beat just until smooth. If necessary, cover and chill until firm enough to spread.

Makes about 1½ cups.

Chocolate Marshmallow Frosting

This silky chocolate concoction is a chocolate lover's sweet dreams come true.

2¼ cups sifted powdered sugar
⅔   cup unsweetened cocoa powder
6   large marshmallows
4   tablespoons (½ stick) butter
5   to 6 tablespoons milk
1   teaspoon pure vanilla extract

• Sift the sugar and cocoa powder together into a large mixing bowl; set aside.

• In a medium, heavy saucepan over low heat combine the marshmallows, butter, and milk. Stir until the marshmallows are melted, 3 to 4 minutes. Remove the pan from the heat. Pour the powdered sugar and cocoa mixture over the marshmallow mixture. Add the vanilla and stir until the frosting is smooth and satiny. Let sit 5–10 minutes to set up slightly before spreading on cookies.

Makes about 1½ cups.

Icings, Frostings, & Other Adornments

Sweetened Whipped Cream

For 1 cup:

½   cup heavy whipping cream
1   tablespoon granulated sugar
½   teaspoon vanilla extract

For 1½ cups:

¾   cup heavy whipping cream
2   tablespoons granulated sugar
1   teaspoon vanilla extract

For 2 cups:

1   cup heavy whipping cream
3   tablespoons granulated sugar
1½ teaspoons vanilla extract

For 3 cups:

1½ cups heavy whipping cream
¼   cup granulated sugar
2   teaspoons vanilla extract

●Beat whipping cream and sugar in chilled mixing bowl with an electric mixer on high speed until soft peaks form. Use immediately.

Glossary of Baking Terms

Beat

To combine ingredients vigorously with a spoon, fork, wire whisk, hand beater, or electric mixer until the ingredients are smooth and uniform.

Blend

To combine ingredients with a spoon, wire whisk, or rubber scraper until very smooth and uniform. A blender or food processor may also be used, depending on the job.

Boil

To heat a liquid until bubbles rise continuously and break on the surface and steam is given off. For a rolling boil, the bubbles form rapidly and will not stop forming even when the liquid is stirred.

Chop

To cut food into small pieces using a chef's knife, food processor, or blender.

Drain

To pour off extra liquid from a food, often with the use of a colander or strainer over the sink. To reserve the drained liquid, place a bowl under the colander.

Drizzle

To slowly pour a liquid mixture, such as butter, chocolate, or glaze, in a very thin stream over a food.

Fold

To combine ingredients lightly while preventing loss of air by using two motions: Using a rubber spatula, first cut down vertically through the mixture. Next, slide the spatula across the bottom of the bowl and up the side, turning the mixture over. Repeat these motions after rotating the bowl one-fourth turn with each series of strokes.

Garnish

An edible decoration added to food.

Grease

To rub the inside surface of a pan with solid shortening, using a pastry brush, wax paper, or paper towels to prevent food from sticking during baking. Nonstick cooking spray may also be used. Do not use butter or margarine (especially in a baked recipe); either may burn and/or sticking may occur.

Grease and Flour

To rub the inside surface of a pan with solid shortening before dusting it with flour in order to prevent food from sticking during baking. After flouring the pan, turn it upside down and tap the bottom to remove excess flour.

Mix

To combine ingredients in any way that distributes them evenly, integrating the ingredients. This can be accomplished using a hand utensil or an electric mixer.

Pipe

A decorating technique that involves forcing frosting, icing, or chocolate from a pastry bag or parchment cone to form specific designs on a cookie.

Preheat

To turn the oven controls to the desired temperature, allowing the oven to heat thoroughly before adding food. Preheating takes about 10-15 minutes.

Set

To allow a food to become firm.

Soften

To allow cold food, such as butter, margarine, or cream cheese, to stand at room temperature until no longer hard. Generally this will take 30–60 minutes.

Stir

To combine ingredients with a circular or "figure 8" motion until they are of a uniform consistency.

Whip

To beat ingredients with a wire whisk, hand rotary beater, or electric mixer to add air and increase volume until ingredients are light and fluffy, such as with whipping cream or egg whites.

Zest

The perfume-y outermost layer of citrus fruit that contains the fruit's essential oils. Zest can be removed with a zester, a small handheld tool that separates the zest from the bitter white pith underneath, or with a grater, vegetable peeler, or sharp knife.

Sources for Ingredients & Equipment

A Best Kitchen

424 West Exchange Street
Akron, Ohio 44302
330-535-2811
www.abestkitchen.com

A Best Kitchen stocks a widespread selection of baking products including pans, silicone cookie sheet liners, decorating kits, cookie presses, molds, cutters, and stamps.

Bridge Kitchenware

214 East 52nd Street
New York, NY 10022
212-274-3435
800-274-3535
www.bridgekitchenware.com

In addition to its wide variety of general cookie-baking equipment and tools, Bridge Kitchenware also offers an extensive selection of cookie sheets.

Bed Bath and Beyond

800-462-3966
www.bedbathandbeyond.com

You might not know it from their name, but Bed Bath and Beyond has an extensive cooking and baking department, complete with appliances (e.g., food processors, toaster/convection ovens, and pizzelle irons), general baking equipment (e.g., pans, measuring cups and spoons, bowls, cookie sheets, cooling racks, and silicone mats), and specific cookie tools (e.g., cutters, stamps, madeleine pans, and decorating kits).

Beryl's Cake Decorating Equipment

P.O. Box 1584
North Springfield, VA 22151
703-256-6951
800-488-2749
www.beryls.com

Beryl's Cake Decorating Equipment is a particularly good source for original cookie cutters and sets.

Chef's Catalog

3215 Commercial Avenue
Northbrook, IL 60062-1900
800-967-2433
www.chefscatalog.com

Cookie sheets, cookie stamps, cookie cutters, multi-decker cooling racks, and just about every other piece of cooking equipment you can imagine is available from Chef's Catalog.

Dean & DeLuca

560 Broadway
New York, NY 10012
212-431-1691
800-221-7714

www.deandeluca.com

Dean & DeLuca carries an upscale assortment of baking tools from spice mills to timers to all manner of goods specific to cookie preparation. They also have cookie ingredient provisions such as imported chocolate, cocoa powder, extracts, and spices.

J.B. Prince Company

36 East 31st Street
New York, NY 10016
212-683-3553
800-473-0577
www.jbprince.com

J.B. Prince Company sells professional-quality baking equipment, mostly imported from Europe.

Kitchen Collectables, Inc.

888-593-2436
www.kitchencollectables.com

No matter what cookie cutter you are looking for, Kitchen Collectables, Inc. is likely to have it. In addition to more than 2,000 copper cookie cutters, they also stock a wide variety of basic and hard-to-find cookie tools and accessories.

King Arthur Flour Baker's Catalog

P.O. Box 876
Norwich, VT 05055
800-827-6836
www.kingarthurflour.com

King Arthur Flour Baker's Catalog offers home bakers a wide range of cookie equipment as well as specialty flours, specialty sugars, and specialty extracts.

Kitchen Krafts

P.O. Box 442-ORD
Waukon, Iowa 52172-0442
563-535-8000
800-776-0575
www.kitchenkrafts.com

Kitchen Krafts is a good one-stop supplier for both basic and fancy cookie and other baking supplies. Especially for novice bakers who need to stock up on basic tools, Kitchen Krafts offers competitive prices on all of their equipment.

La Cuisine

323 Cameron Street
Alexandria, VA 22314
703-836-4435
800-521-1176
www.lacuisineus.com

In addition to all of the basic cookie baking equipment you may need, La Cuisine also carries cookie decorations, including specialty decorating sugars.

Lamalle Kitchenware

36 West 25th Street
New York, NY 10010
212-242-0750
www.foodnet.com/epr/sections/writers/trends/lamall.html

Lamalle's is the source for unique cutters and other specialty cookie tools.

Parrish's Cake Decorating Supplies, Inc.

225 West 16th Street
Gardena, CA 90248-1803
310-324-2253
800-736-8443
www.parrishsmagicline.com/sys-tmpl/door

Parrish's is "cookie baking central," offering a wide variety of cookie equipment, including cutters, presses, molds, and other cookie tools.

Penzey's Spices

P.O. Box 993
W129362 Apollo Drive
Muskego, WI 53150
800-741-7787
www.penzeys.com

Look to Penzey's for some of the best and freshest spices at good prices. They also carry assorted extracts and are an especially good source for hard-to-find spices and flavorings.

Sources for Ingredients and Equipment

Sur La Table

1765 Sixth Avenue South
Seattle, WA 93134-1608
800-243-0852
www.surlatable.com

Sur La Table has a wide selection of baking equipment and appliances in general and cookie baking and decorating supplies in particular. They also carry a wide variety of fine baking ingredients, including imported chocolates and pure chocolate and vanilla extracts.

Sweet Celebrations

P.O. Box 39426
Edina, MN 55439-0426
612-943-0426
800-328-6722
www.maidofscandinavia.com

Sweet Celebrations carries a wide range of cake decorating supplies, baking equipment, and imported chocolate for baking.

Williams-Sonoma

P.O. Box 7456
San Francisco, CA 94120-7456
415-421-4242
800-541-2233
www.williams-sonoma.com

Williams-Sonoma offers a wide range of baking equipment, including, but not limited to, appliances (mixers, food processors, and combined toaster-convection ovens), cookie accessories (cutters, presses, sheets, silicone liners, cake and cookie decorating tips), and ingredients (decorating sugar and imported chocolate, cocoa, and vanilla).

Wilton Enterprises, Inc.

240 West 75th Street
Woodbridge, IL 60517
630-963-7100
800-794-5866
www.wilton.com

In addition to being a leading cake decoration supplier, Wilton Enterprises also carries an extensive selection of cookie cutters and most every other type of cookie baking accessory, from presses to molds to stamps. They also stock a wide variety of decorating accessories, including pastry bags and tips.

Metric Conversions

Note: The exact amounts of these measurements have been rounded for the sake of convenience.

Liquid and Dry Measures

U.S.	Metric
¼ teaspoon	1.25 milliliters
½ teaspoon	2.5 milliliters
1 teaspoon	5 milliliters
1 tablespoon	15 milliliters
1 fluid ounce	30 milliliters
¼ cup (4 tbsp)	60 milliliters
⅓ cup	80 milliliters
1 cup (16 tbsp)	240 milliliters
1 pint (2 cups)	480 milliliters
1 quart (4 cups)	960 milliliters
1 gallon (4 qts)	3.84 milliliters

Length Measures

U.S.	Metric
⅛ inch	3 millimeters
¼ inch	6 millimeters
½ inch	12 millimeters
1 inch	25 millimeters

Oven Temperatures

Fahrenheit	Celsius
300	150
325	160
350	180
375	190
400	200
425	220
450	475
475	240
500	260

Index

Index